Plays: 1

The Street of Crocodiles, The Three Lives of Lucie Cabrol, Mnemonic

The Street of Crocodiles: '. . . has a lightness of texture that perfectly counterpoints the underlying gravity of the Bruno Schulz stories on which it is based . . .' Michael Billington, *Guardian*

The Three Lives of Lucie Cabrol: 'You follow this Complicite version [of John Berger's story] as intensely as you would read a Grimms' fairytale.' Alastair Macaulay, *Financial Times*

Mnemonic 'connects the seemingly unconnected: past with present, you and me, the songs we share, the stories we once told and the stories we tell now.' Lyn Gardner, *Guardian*

Founded in 1983, Complicite is a constantly evolving ensemble of performers and collaborators, now led by Artistic Director Simon McBurney. Complicite's work has ranged from entirely devised work to theatrical adaptations and revivals of classic texts. The Company has also worked in other media; a radio production of *Mnemonic* for BBC Radio 3, collaborations with John Berger on a radio adaptation of his novel *To The Wedding* for BBC Radio and *The Vertical Line*, a multi-disciplinary installation performed in a disused tube station, commissioned by Artangel. Always changing and moving forward to incorporate new stimuli, the principles of the work have remained close to the original impulses: seeking what is most alive, integrating text, music, image and action to create surprising, disruptive theatre.

COMPLICITE

Plays: 1

The Street of Crocodiles

The Three Lives of Lucie Cabrol

Mnemonic

Introduced by Simon McBurney

Methuen Drama

METHUEN CONTEMPORARY DRAMATISTS

Published by Methuen 2003

1 3 5 7 9 10 8 6 4 2

First published in 2003 by
Methuen Publishing Limited,
215 Vauxhall Bridge Road,
London SW1V 1EJ

The Street of Crocodiles first published in 1999 by Methuen Publishing Ltd
The Three Lives of Lucie Cabrol first published in 1995 by Methuen Publishing Ltd
Mnemonic first published in 1999 by Methuen Publishing Ltd

Methuen Publishing Limited Reg. No. 3543167

A CIP catalogue record for this book is available from the British Library.

ISBN 0 413 77383 3

Typeset by SX Composing DTP, Rayleigh, Essex
Printed and bound in Great Britain by
Cox and Wyman Ltd, Reading, Berkshire

Caution

Contents

A Chronology

Prologue

Three plays are gathered in this book – *The Street of Crocodiles*, *The Three Lives of Lucie Cabrol* and *Mnemonic*. They are in many ways quite separate in time, space, meaning and style. The world of *The Street of Crocodiles* is that of the unconscious and the imagination. The short stories by Polish Jewish writer, Bruno Schulz, which form the inspiration for the piece, describe small town life in Galicia at the end of the Austro-Hungarian Empire seen through the eyes of a child. The play is constructed of fragments from these stories. Fleeting, apparently random images and fragmentary scenes evoke pungent feelings and imply a story; but it is one that is never made explicit. People drift across the lost world of a small town in turn-of-the-century Poland, turning the stage into a dreamscape. By contrast, in *The Three Lives of Lucie Cabrol*, John Berger confronts us with unflinching reality. It is the story of a peasant woman born in the Haut Savoie in 1900 and describes a pitiless life of bone-breaking physical labour in the French Alps. The narrative is direct, explicit and moves relentlessly towards its tragic conclusion. In *Mnemonic*, there are multiple stories. Five contemporary stories set in different countries and spanning thousands of years are interwoven, unfolding at the same time in the same space.

In all of the pieces, we are far from a reality that we might think of as 'ours'. The subject matter, a pre-war Polish-Jewish upbringing, the life of poor mountain peasants and an archaeological discovery dating back 33,000 years does not strike us now as personal and intimate. Yet, for me, somehow that is what they are – both intimate and personal. Perhaps it is that they are all to do with memory, people remembering things. In *The Street of Crocodiles* Joseph remembers when he smells the book he is reading. For Jean in *Lucie Cabrol*, it is the heat of the fire which brings back the dead and in *Mnemonic* the physical sensation of being alone in your room in the middle of the night unable to sleep, produces the cascade of memories and associations about love and loss. The physical stimulation of memory is a general human experience, common to us all, but it evokes something that is unique to each of us. It defines who we are in life and is also our point of contact with the dead. My mother was a birdwatcher. Months after she died, my arm would move involuntarily to the telephone when I saw a heron fly over my house.

There is another reason why they belong together; why they are side by side in this book. It is because of the way they were made. They are all compositional pieces that came about through a process of collaboration. The work of Bruno Schulz, John Berger and the story of the Iceman, as recounted by Konrad Spindler, were the starting points in each case. From there they were developed through chaotic and continually evolving rehearsals that involved improvisation, argument, writing, rewriting, despair and hope. They represent the work of more than fifty people, coming together over a period of seven years. They were developed as they were performed. And they have been performed in countries all over the world to audiences who then influence the way we remake the shows the next time we play. With each change, be they new actors, new technicians, new producers or new audiences, fresh insights emerge, new directions are discovered and pointed out. In this way, the pieces have become meeting points, destinations, points de départs, we could even say they have become places in themselves.

All the pieces are about a common sense of dis-placement. An experience of loss, of a kind of banishment specific to our time. *Lucie Cabrol* charts not only her exile from the village, but her adaptation to being banished from a way of life that has been in place almost unchanged since the Neolithic age. For Bruno Schulz, the vanished world of his childhood stands as a metaphor for all that was disappearing in that part of the world, the end of empire and the shock of twentieth century commercialisation. The gathering darkness in the stories also prophesies all that was to be obliterated after his death. And in *Mnemonic*, the parallel stories of searching for a father and searching to uncover a more distant death, that of the Iceman, serve to focus a common desire to know 'Where do I come from?'

In the past a sense of belonging was obtained through a continuity of history and the unchanging nature of place. Those who were stationary tended to think of the experience of displacement belonging to the emigrant. But as I have travelled and performed it seems to me that this sensation of 'homelessness' – of a rupture with the past, a kind of dismantling of history and experience – is not only that of the emigrant, forced through economic, social and political violence to tear up all that is known and move to start a new life elsewhere. It seems, now, to be a common experience, a product of our time. Perhaps it is best described as a loss of continuity between the past and the future; a loss of connection between our dead and those yet to be born. And, perhaps, this sensation of loss is what brought the people who made these pieces to the same space, the site of these plays. It is one of the things that has joined us with audiences everywhere.

'Why do you need to know about your father?' Virgil asks Alice in the final scene of *Mnemonic*.

'Because if I don't know who he is, I feel I can't come home,' she replies.

'Then imagine,' says Virgil.

Perhaps in some small way this is an answer. That is to say the act of collective imagination itself creates a site.

What can grow on this site of loss? It is strange to suggest that these pieces are something as static as a 'site', since they are constantly shifting and moving. As are the people involved in their creation. So if they are 'sites' or places in themselves then they are places of passage. Passing places. Such as you find on single track roads in the mountains. When a driver travelling in the opposite direction is forced to give way to allow both to continue their journeys, there is a curiously intimate moment of contact as one waits and the other passes. What is marvellous is not the passing but what passes between; passed through the look, the acknowledgement, the gesture. And travelling with these pieces to many places in the world it is this which creates a sense of belonging. What passes between. The pieces become part of a kind of nomad hospitality. As a collaborator I have constantly received this hospitality from my fellow makers, and as a performer it is something I have received from audiences everywhere. This is why I can feel at home almost anywhere. It is also why I feel I can go on.

This is not simply a personal phenomenon but also reflects and expresses the time we are living in. The feeling of rupture is being modified, maybe transcended by a new sense of intimacy across great distances. To simply call it communication is to underestimate it. It is a passing of secrets. In the same way our forebears attended to the essential needs that gave meaning to their lives, perhaps we need to give this passing communication the same quality of attention – the attention that was once given to the eternal.

I am writing this sitting in the window on the first floor, looking down at a path of boulders set in a garden of gravel. The path leads to a teahouse that has been constructed on the trunk of a tree. I am in Japan. Kyoto. I recognise none of the plants. I do not know the metaphoric significance of the arch of grass or the stone carvings; nothing I can see is familiar to me. Yet curiously, although I am here in passing, I feel completely at home. And when I see something that looks like a heron, I still reach for the phone . . .

Here in Japan, in what are surroundings that could not be further from my own life, staying with people who speak as little English as I do Japanese, I have a sense of belonging. I am here because when my hosts saw *The Street of Crocodiles* some years ago their response was to invite us to their house, which is a temple in Kyoto. Messages from everywhere come here.

Which is why this book is dedicated to all those who have in any way participated in the creation of these pieces – those passing, and those who have become eternal.

Simon McBurney
May 2003

The Street of Crocodiles

Dedicated to Jacob Schulz who died in 1997.

Bruno Schulz: a chronology

1892   12 July: Bruno Schulz born in Drohobycz, East Galicia, a province of the Austro-Hungarian Empire. His father was a Jewish shopkeeper.

1902–10 Bruno attends a school named after Emperor Francis Joseph. But he does not grow up in the dominant traditions of German-speaking Austria. Nor does he remain in the sphere of traditional Jewish culture, his parents being assimilated Jews. He never learned Yiddish; he knew German but he spoke and wrote in Polish.

1905–15 With his father an invalid, Bruno spends all his free time at his father's bedside.

1911–13 Bruno studies at the Academy of Art in Vienna then goes on to the University of Lvov to study Architecture.

After the First World War, Poland is created a republic. Galicia is annexed by the republic in 1921.

1915-24 Years Bruno describes as his 'lost, stupid and idle youth'. He spends most of his time reading and drawing.

1924   Bruno begins teaching at a local high school, his earnings supporting his mother, his sister and her son. His classes are, for Bruno, an unwelcome distraction from the main business of his life – his writings and drawings. His pupils later recall the fabulous stories he told and illustrated with a few swift lines on the board or on pieces of paper.

1930   Bruno publishes a book of drawings, *The Book of Idolatory*.

1932   Bruno has a one-man show of drawings and paintings in Lvov. It is a qualified success.

1934   *Cinnamon Shops*, Bruno's first book of stories, is published to wide acclaim. It is very successful and gains him the recognition and friendships he has long desired. It also brings controversy. The headmaster of the high school forbids his pupils to read it and declares it an 'abomination, a scandal that profanes the Polish language'.

1937   Bruno's book, *Sanatorium under the Sign of the Hourglass*, is published with illustrations by the author. He also translates *The Trial* by Kafka.

1938   Bruno works on his masterpiece, *The Messiah*. Though various sections of it were entrusted to the safekeeping of friends, none of it, to our knowledge, has survived.

17 September 1940: The German army enters Drohobycz.
Winter 1940: The Soviet army enters Drohobycz.
1941 onwards: Drohobycz under German occupation.

1941   Bruno is forced to leave his job at the high school. He offers his services as a draughtsman to the Third Reich and is refused. He is protected by a Nazi officer, Felix Landau, as a 'useful Jew'. He paints Landau's portrait.

1942: Ghetto confinement is enforced.

1942   Bruno and a fellow Jew, a solicitor, Izydor Freidmen, are employed to catalogue books for the Nazis in order that those the Nazis consider worthwhile may be exported to Germany. Bruno's friends draw up an elaborate plan of escape.

19 November 1942: The Nazis kill 150 Jews in retaliation for the shooting of a Nazi officer.

A few days earlier, Landau had shot a Jew under the protection of a rival officer. This officer takes advantage of what later becomes known as 'Black Thursday' to search Bruno out and shoot him twice in the head. 'You shot my Jew, so I shot yours.'

1957   Bruno's stories are reissued in Polish and translated into German and French and begin to find an international readership.

Note on the script

The present version of this script has been developed steadily since the project of *The Street of Crocodiles* began at the Royal National Theatre Studio in 1991. Eight years after the journey began, it is still migrating, developing and changing. Along with the original cast, we have included in this volume a list of people who have been part of that journey, most especially Jacob Schulz, Bruno's nephew, who died in 1997 and to whom this text is dedicated. For us Jacob formed the link between the present and the living past.

The script originated with the short stories of Bruno Schulz, collected in two volumes entitled *Cinnamon Shops* and *Sanatorium Under the Sign of the Hourglass*. Because they deviate from the normal rules of narrative and eschew superficial drama, our process was as much one of invention as adaptation (to this end, we have included quotations which will point the reader to the textual inspiration at the origin of each scene). Our process involved not only the writing of original dialogue (as with any play) but also the lifting of text direct from the stories (and from Schulz's letters and essays). We used descriptions of him given to us by Jacob. We worked on improvisations in which the actors played out the process of memory which lies at the heart of all his stories. We recreated the atmosphere of his times and the mechanism of his dreams. We investigated the rhythm of his nightmares and his intense engagement with his beloved and despised solitude.

If you had opened the door of the rehearsal room when we first began you might have thought you were in a prop maker's workshop, a second-hand clothes store, or even a hallucinatory jam session, with the participants playing desks instead of drums and dancing with coats instead of partners. We used anything which came to hand to find a landmark and open up directions in which to travel. We read the stories over and over, improvised and argued. We went up blind alleys, losing ourselves in Schulz's vast imaginative landscapes and the mazes of his fantasy. For to spend time in his company turns your head ('*Dizzy with light, we dip into the enormous book of holidays, its pages scented with the sweet melting pulp of golden pears*'). The sensuality of his writing captures those long forgotten smells from the past, with an imagination that can transform gazing at a stamp album into a religious trauma ('*Canada, Honduras, Nicaragua, Abracadabra, Hipporabundia . . . I at last understood you, oh God!*').

So, this book is more the record of a process than a text for performance; a map rather than a play. A play is a place which demands to be inhabited; both origin and destination, linked by a clearly determined path. A map indicates the landscape, suggests a multitude of directions, but does not dictate which one you should take. A map, however beautiful, is a guide not a site. If you wish to visit the site yourself, pick up Schulz's books. And travel.

Simon McBurney and Mark Wheatley,
January 1999

The Street of Crocodiles, originally a co-production with the
Royal National Theatre, was first performed at the
Cottesloe Theatre, London on 6 August 1992. In 1992 and
1993 it toured to: the Sydney Festival; Gracie Fields
Theatre, Rochdale; Tramway, Glasgow; Oxford Playhouse;
Theatre Royal, Winchester; Cambridge Arts Theatre;
Dundee Repertory Theatre; Traverse Edinburgh; Theater
Gessner Allee, Zurich; LIFE Festival, Vilnius; Tagenka
Theatre, Moscow; Theatr Polski, Wroclaw; Israel Festival,
Jerusalem; Theater der Welt, Munich; and Grec Festival,
Barcelona.

A 1994 revival toured to: National Theatre, Bucharest;
Muvesz Szinhaz, Budapest; Festival Theatre en Mai, Dijon;
Carrefour International, Quebec; Bonner Biennale, Cologne;
Reykjavik Arts Festival; Theatre du Merlan, Marseille; the
Dublin Theatre Festival; Festival de Otono, Madrid; Gardner
Arts Centre, Brighton; Young Vic, London; and Whitehall
Theatre, London.

A revival in 1998 toured with a new cast to: Lincoln
Center Festival, New York; Toronto Harbourfront Centre;
Minneapolis Theatre de la Jeune Lune; and Setagaya Public
Theatre, Tokyo. 1999 West End season at the Queens
Theatre, London and Stockholm, Stadsteater.

Based on the stories of Bruno Schulz
Adapted by Simon McBurney & Mark Wheatley
Devised by The Company

Director Simon McBurney
Design Rae Smith
Lighting Paule Constable
Sound Christopher Shutt

The original cast was as follows:

Joseph	Cesar Sarachu
Father (Jacob)	Matthew Scurfield
Mother (Henrietta)	Annabel Arden
The Family:	

Uncle Charles	Clive Mendus
Agatha	Joyce Henderson
Cousin Emil	Antonio Gil Martinez
The Maids:	
Adela	Lilo Baur
Maria	Hayley Carmichael
The Shop Assistants:	
Theodore	Eric Mallett
Leon	Stefan Metz

1994 Revival

Cast Annabel Arden, Lilo Baur, Hayley Carmichael, Antonio Gil Martinez, Joyce Henderson, Eric Mallett, Clive Mendus, Stefan Metz, Cesar Sarachu, Matthew Scurfield

1998–9 Revival

Cast Annabel Arden, Bronagh Gallagher, Eric Mallett, Antonio Gil Martinez, Gregory Gudgeon, Marcello Magni, Charlotte Medcalf, Clive Mendus, Stefan Metz, Cesar Sarachu, Matthew Scurfield, Ásta Sighvats

Awards

1993   Four Olivier Award nominations for: BBC Award for Best Play, Best Director, Best Lighting, Best Choreography (Marcello Magni)
1993   Barcelona Critics Award for Best Foreign Production
1993   Manchester *Evening Standard* Award for Best Visiting Production
1994   L'Academie Quebecoise du Théâtre Award for Best Foreign Production
1994   Dublin Theatre Festival Award for Best Visiting Production

Thanks to all those who have contributed to the production over the years: Paul Anderson, Anita Ashwick, Simon Auton, Dave Ball, Jason Barnes, Sophie Brech, Chris Chibnall, Nobby Clark, Johanna Coe, Claudia Courtis, Susan Croft,

Christina Cunningham, Henrietta Duckworth, Judith Edgely, Sandra Formica, Gareth Fry, Sue Gibbs, Paddy Hamilton, Sue Higginson & the NT Studio, Sarah-Jane Hughes, Johnny Hutch, Helena Kaut-Howson, Irene Kozica, Jacek Laskowski, Helen Lewis, Peter Lewis, John Mackinnon, Gerard McBurney, Richard McDougall, Pete McPhail, Rosa Maggiora, Marcello Magni, Jane Martin, Nadia Morgan, Oxford Museum of Modern Art, Naomi Parker, Picador Books, Marek Podostolski, The Polish Cultural Institute, Quay Brothers, Catherine Reiser, Ian Richards, Lorraine Richards, Martin Riley, Doug Rintoul, Richard Rudznicki, Red Saunders, Jacob Schulz, Danusia Stok, Gemma Swallow, Judith Thorpe, Steve Wald, Russell Warren-Fisher, Ed Wilson, Octavia Wiseman, Ray Wolf.

Note

As many of the actors were from different countries, you will find in the script that they speak in their own languages.

The quotations from Bruno Schulz's work come from *The Collected Works of Bruno Schulz*, published by Picador.

Prologue

The sorting of books

As a Jew, I was assigned by the Drohobycz Judenrat to work in a library under Gestapo authority, and so was Schulz. This was a depository made up of all public and the major private libraries . . . the books were to be catalogued or committed to destruction by Schulz and myself. *Letter to Jerzy Ficowksi from Tadeusz Lubowiecki, Gilwice, 1949.*

A warehouse on the outskirts of Drohobycz in Poland. 19 November 1942. Through the half dark, piles of discarded books are highlighted by spotlights.

The sound of dripping water as the audience enter the mist-filled auditorium.

Joseph *enters USL double doors. He takes off his coat and hangs it on the back wall. As he crosses DSR he looks at the bucket to see where the dripping is coming from. Exits DSR double doors.*

Voice (*off*) He du, komm her! Sortier die neue Ladung Bücher und schmeiss den Schund weg!

Joseph (*off*) Ja, ja . . .

Voice (*off*) Los, los, beweg dich!

Joseph *returns with books pushed in a packing case with wheels. He is sorting and cataloguing books. He has a pen and a sheaf of bookmarks. He writes on them and puts them in the books that are to be kept. These he takes up the ladder left and places in a row. The others he drops on the floor. One book he holds longer than others as if reluctant to commit it to destruction.*

Voice (*off*) Ja, das ist die letzte Ladung . . . die letzte, hab' ich gesagt!

Joseph *drops the book in his fright and then carries on the sorting. He finds another book particularly appealing. He is unable to throw it away. He stops, and looks at it. Out of it falls a feather. He takes a chair DSC and begins to read.*

The sound of marching feet.

Joseph *stands and watches them pass. He sits on his chair again, opens the book again. He smells its pages.*

Music.

Part One: Act of Remembrance

1 The summoning of the past

Somewhere in the dawn of childhood was The Book; the wind would rustle through its pages and the pictures would rise. Page after page floated in the air and gently saturated the landscape with brightness. *The Book*

The cast gradually appear on stage as if called up by **Joseph***'s imagination. One of* **Father***'s assistants,* **Theodore***, walks down the wall perpendicular to the audience, pauses to take his hat and looks up as, out of the bucket, his twin assistant,* **Leon***, appears – wet and dripping. Having struggled out of the small bucket, he picks it up. There is no trace of where he has come from.* **Maria** *emerges from the packing case of books.* **Charles, Emil** *and* **Agatha** *emerge from behind bookcases.* **Mother***, swathed in cloth, shuffles forward on her knees with a book covered in a shawl. At a signal, they all produce books in their hands and look at* **Joseph***.*

Joseph   And there are rooms which are sometimes forgotten . . .

Father (*appears*)   And there are rooms which are sometimes forgotten. Unvisited for months on end, they wilt, become overgrown with bricks and lost once and for all to our memory, forfeit their only claim to existence. Once, early in the morning towards the end of winter, I visted such a forgotten chamber. From all the crevices in the floor, from all the mouldings, from every recess there grew slim shoots filling the grey air with a scintillating filigree lace of leaves. Around the bed, under the lamp, along the wardrobes clumps of delicate trees, which high above spread their luminous crowns, enormous white and pink flowers blossomed among the leaves, bursting with bud before your very eyes, and then falling apart in quick decay. And before nightfall there is no trace left of that splendid flowering. The whole elusive sight was a *fata morgana*, an example of the

strange make-believe of matter which had created a
semblance of life.

They all proceed and sit on chairs.

   Adela   Father   Leon   Theodore   Charles

Mother

Maria

Emil

Agatha

2   The awakening of memory

Who can understand the great and sad machinery of spring? Tree
roots want to speak, freshly starched underskirts rustle on park
benches, and stories are rejuvenated and start their plots again.
Spring

At the age of eight, Bruno's mother read to him Goethe's
'Erlkönig', of which he said later: 'Through half-understood
German, I felt its sense and was shattered and wept deeply.' *Notes
to the company from Jacob Schulz, Bruno's nephew, June 1992*

Joseph *turns and sees them. He seems to remember these people.
They are relics of his memory, a little broken down and faded. He turns
back front and they rise one by one as if attached to him. They form the
shape of a class behind him with chairs only and sit as he sits. They
begin reciting the first lines of 'Der Erlkönig'.*

Mother
'Wer reitet so spät durch Nacht und Wind?'

All
'Es ist der Vater mit seinem Kind.'

Agatha
'Er hat den Knaben wohl in dem Arm.'

Maria
'Er fasst ihn sicher' . . .

Adela
> . . . 'er halt ihn warm.'

Joseph *looks behind him. He is surprised to see these people. He looks away. They laugh and form themselves into little groups, as if at tables in an open-air café courtyard. He looks back. These are the groups behind him:* **Agatha**, **Charles** *and* **Emil** *left.* **Leon**, **Theodore** *and* **Adela** *right.* **Mother** *and* **Father** *USR.* **Maria** *centre.*

Joseph (*begins walking round them*)   Theodore? (*Goes to* **Theodore** *and takes his coat.*)

Theodore   Leon! Psst! (*Gets up.* **Leon** *follows him.*)

Joseph   Leon?

They cross to **Emil** *and take his coat.* **Joseph** *watches them.*

Adela (*calls from behind* **Joseph***'s back*)   Joseph!

Joseph   Adela?

Adela   My God, Joseph, you're as thin as a rake.

Joseph *turns back to* **Leon** *and* **Theodore** *as he hears them laugh and sees . . .*

Joseph   Emil?

Emil   Hombre Joseph! Pero que allegria, chico! How wonderful to see you . . . (*He takes* **Joseph** *centre stage, behind his chair.*) You've changed, you're a man now! Un hombre! Joseph did I ever tell you what I saw in Madagascar? (*Takes him behind the chairs of* **Charles** *and* **Agatha**.) In Madagascar I found these photos; fotografias de chicas desnuditas.

Agatha *tries to look.* **Emil** *points to distract her attention.*

Mira qué tetitas. Son las chicas de Madagas-*car*. (*His voice cracks on the last syllable. He tries again.*) Madagas-*car*. (*Same result.*)

Charles *tries to help by tuning the syllable to the highest note of the banjo.*

Madgas-*car*. (*Same result. More tuning.*) . . . -car-car-car . . .
(*Still the voice cracks.*)

Charles *has a new idea. He plays the four strings of the banjo to try
and achieve the desired result.*

Emil (*tries to sing it*) Mad-da-gas-car (*Same result.*) . . . -car-
car-car . . . (*Shakes his head.*)

Father   Joseph! How extraordinary!

Joseph   Father!

Father   Even these wild and spacious late winter skies are
transformed . . .

*The books carried by the characters begin to flutter and change into
birds, gathering in a flock DSR and then crossing DSL.*

. . . by the arrival of returning birds . . . look . . . look flying
hither and thither within the lap of eternal matter.

The birds flit around him in preventing **Joseph** *from seeing his father.*

Joseph   Oh Father, Father . . . Mother!

Mother   Joseph . . . Spring!

The group rises and puts chairs above their heads. We are in a wood.

The sound of birds.

Mother   What is it in the air of a spring dusk? Old trees
regain their sweetness and wake up their twigs and yet there
are so many whispers which lie buried underground and are
forgotten. Who can understand that great and sad
machinery of spring? The tree roots want to speak,
memories awake, ah Joseph, freshly starched underskirts
and new silk stockings rustle on park benches, their stories
are rejuvenated and start their plots again. But others
remain unborn and beautiful spring lives vicariously on the
rejected lives of unborn tales.

Mother *has disappeared.*

Joseph   Mother, Mother . . .

Maria *appears coming DSL to stand in front of* **Joseph**.

Joseph (*goes to* **Maria**. *He does not know what to say*.)
Spring!

There is a shocked intake of breath from the wood. They raise their chairs.

Maria   Yes.

The chairs breathe out. They descend in a kind of relief. The ice has been broken.

Joseph   The stars . . . look, a shooting star!

Maria *brings out half a plate and shows it to him.*

Joseph   The moon!

Maria   No!

Joseph   Yes!

Maria   No! I'm looking for my other half. (*She indicates the other half of the plate.*)

Joseph (*he doesn't have it*)   Well . . . I'm sorry.

Maria *gets up and runs round the wood.*

Joseph (*following her*)   Hey, señorita, hey, señorita, please wait! Wait!

Maria *stops by* **Adela** *and takes her chair.* **Joseph** *pursues* **Adela**. **Adela** *stops and turns on him.*

Adela   Joseph!

Joseph   Adela?

Adela   Joseph, what are you doing out so late?

Joseph (*he is confused*)   Adela? Adela?

He stops and touches one of the trees. It falls. The other trees fall.

Joseph   My God, these people.

Maria (*stands up*)   Joseph.

Joseph   Hey, señorita!

Everyone stands up quickly and **Maria** *continues to run round.*

Mother   Joseph, look! The moon! The moon!

Maria *picks up the group as she goes.*

Joseph   Yes, the moon, Mother!

The group stops DSR.

Charles   Joseph, the stars!

Joseph   Yes, the stars!

Leon   Ist das nicht wunderschön?

The group run through **Joseph** *USL.* **Joseph** *pursues* **Maria** *and grabs her. Her coat comes off and she disappears into the group.*

Joseph   Señorita, please tell me, what's your name?

The group cross around **Joseph** *to DSR and disappear.*

Agatha/Group   Joseph!

Joseph *strokes the coat with his face. The vision has disappeared but the coat tells him it was more than an imagining. He places it in the packing case and goes back to his book DSC. He looks into his book and up again.*

Part Two: The Age of Genius

1 The class

Dear and respected friend . . . School today is not the school of an
earlier day . . . teaching a likeable gang of twenty-six boys
equipped with hammers, saws and planes, is an honourable
struggle, and the violent and desperate measures of intimidation I
must resort to in order to keep them in check fill me with disgust.
Extract from a letter from Bruno Schulz to Wacław Czarski, Chief Editor of
Tygodnik Illustrowany (Polish Illustrated Weekly), Winter 1934/35

I am very much worn out by school – I now teach in grade school
– I wish I could get on without a position and live for my writing
alone. *Letter to Romana Halpern, Drohobycz, 1936*

There is no dead matter. Lifelessness, Emil, is only a disguise
behind which lie unknown forms of life. Wood is alive.
Tailor's Dummies

The USL double doors fly open. The class are there cramming the
doorway with desks and chairs. As excited children, they shake their
way to CS and place themselves in a classroom formation.

Father	Mother	Charles
Two assistants	Maria	Agatha
Adela	Joseph	Emil

Joseph (*not sure what he is supposed to teach today*)   Today's
class is . . . (*He goes to the empty crate and looks into it.*) Today's
class is . . . woodwork!

He takes wood from the crate and goes round the class distributing it.
The class have their woodworking tools in their desks. They get them
out and begin working as he goes round.

Emil.

Emil   China, Guatemala and Madagascar . . .

Joseph   Very good, Emil . . . Agatha.

Agatha *drops her piece of wood.*

Joseph   Be careful Agatha.

Agatha   Careful. (*She drops the piece of wood again.*)

Joseph   Agatha, careful.

Agatha   Careful.

Joseph   Maria . . . Maria. Where are your tools? Your tools!

Agatha *starts to bang on her desk.*

Joseph   Agatha!

Agatha   Just a little bit more.

This annoys **Emil** *so much, he decides to help* **Agatha** *with her banging.*

Emil   Like this! (*Shows her by banging with his own hammer.*)

The desk collapses. **Emil**, *mortified returns to his own desk.*

Agatha   Careful!

Joseph   Agatha, Emil what are you doing?

Emil   Rabbit brain!

Joseph   Quiet please. Go and get another desk! Hurry up! And be quiet Emil, please.

Emil *and* **Agatha** *exit to get another desk.* **Charles** *stabs the piece of wood* **Joseph** *puts down in front of him.*

Adela   Maria . . . cigarette

Joseph   Adela, quiet please . . . quiet

Leon *and* **Theodore** *play an imaginary violin and applaud.* **Adela** *pushes them over.* **Joseph** *is losing control.* **Adela** *tickles* **Father.** **Joseph** *scolds her and sends her back to her seat.*

Joseph   Adela, would you be so kind as to take your piece of wood please?

Adela *pushes the wood away from her teacher.*

Joseph   Adela.

He touches her on the cheek. It is the first sign of his fascination with her. He goes on to the next desk. **Theodore** *and* **Leon** *pretend to play dead.*

Leon . . . Theodore . . . Henrietta . . . (*gives wood to* **Father**) and Jacob!

Father   Crucified timbers! Who knows how many suffering, crippled forms of life there are? Such as the artificially created lives of chests and tables quickly nailed together. Lifelessness, Emil, is only a disguise within which lie unknown forms of life. Yes! Wood is alive. Wood is alive!

Emil*'s wood, which he has dropped on to the floor, leaps back into his hands. Everyone else wants to try this out. Wood and tools and chairs fall everywhere.*

Mother (*standing on her chair*)   Somebody shut him up! Somebody shut him up!

Father   How much ancient suffering is there in the varnished grain of our old familiar wardrobes?

Joseph   Jacob, Jacob, please be quiet and sit down. Jacob! Let's work, please. Very good, Charles. That's it.

He indicates to **Maria** *to put her coat away. He then goes to* **Adela***'s desk and oversees some work between* **Theodore** *and* **Leon***. They bang on one end of a piece of wood. The other falls off. Meanwhile, USC,* **Mother** *and* **Charles** *nail* **Father***'s hand to some wood.*

Oh my God, Jacob, show me your hand.

Father *puts his hand behind his back. When he brings it out, the nail has gone. Everyone is playing tricks on* **Joseph***.*

Father   How much ancient suffering is there . . .

Joseph   Jacob . . . Henrietta you should know better . . . (*He goes round the class settling them down. He finds* **Charles** *at*

Agatha*'s desk*.) Charles what are you doing there? But your place is here. (*He gives up*.)

Emil *raises his hand*.

Joseph   Yes, Emil.

Emil   Madagascar and Hipporabundia!

Joseph   Very good Emil, thank you. (*Indicates his chair to sit down*.)

Emil   Guatemala!

Joseph   Very good, Emil.

Emil   Hipporabundia!

Joseph   Emil, please sit down.

Emil   Uganda, Tanganika and Mozambique!

Joseph   Emil, please . . .

Emil   Paraguay, Uruguay, Venezuela!

Joseph   EMIL!

Emil *sits down contritely.* **Joseph** *sits down.* **Theodore** *and* **Leon** *play with* **Adela**, *singing a little song, to the tune of 'Daisy, Daisy'.*

Assistants
  Adela, Adela, give us your answer do.

Joseph   Shh . . . Shhhh. (*Begins to go to sleep*.)

Assistants (*quietly*)
  We're half crazy, all for the love of you.
  It won't be a stylish marriage,
  We can't afford the carriage,
  But we'll look sweet upon the seat
  Of a bicycle made for two.

Adela *has had enough. She turns and lifts her skirt at them. She gets a glass out of her desk and goes to the tap.* **Joseph** *goes to sleep DSC.*

Charles Agatha . . . (*Blows sawdust in* **Agatha**'*s face.*)

Agatha Charles . . . (*Takes a hammer and hits his thumb.*)

Charles *puts up his hand to appeal to* **Joseph** *at this injustice.*
Joseph *does not respond.* **Adela**, *at the tap drinking water, notices*
Joseph *is asleep. She creeps back to her desk. She drops a piece of*
wood to see if it will wake him up. The whole class follows suit,
banging furiously. **Joseph** *remains asleep. The class hatch a plan.*
Charles *makes a wooden spoon with* **Leon** *and* **Theodore**. *He*
leads the sleeping **Joseph** *round the classroom in a dance of death, the*
class providing the rhythmical accompaniment. **Joseph** *ends by*
standing on a chair in the middle of the room. **Agatha** '*shoots*' *him.*
Joseph *staggers to his chair. The class approach, tapping a sinister*
rhythm. He wakes up. He looks round at the class to see if it was a
dream. The class behave as if everything were normal. But they are now
out of control. They start shifting around the desks. **Joseph** *cannot*
bring them back to their original positions. They suddenly stop.
Joseph *looks at Jacob. He realises that it is his* **Father**.

Father How much ancient suffering is there in the
varnished grain of our old familiar wardrobes?

Joseph Father –

Unable to believe this dreamlike transformation, he goes to the tap to
put cold water on his face.

2 The shop of childhood memory

Childhood . . . oh that invasion of brightness, that blissful spring,
oh, Father . . . *The Book*

The class move their desks around as they work gradually forming them
into a shop counter, ready for the next scene. **Joseph** *looks up from*
the tap. The noise stops and the desks, in a line, conceal the cast. The
tap drips. He turns back to it and stops it. He moves towards the desks,
looking at his **Father**. *As he does so, a bell rings. It is the door to the*
shop. He tries opening the imaginary door. A bell rings again. He
walks into the shop and sees it is his **Father**'*s shop which he*
remembers from his earliest childhood. He goes to his **Father**, *pushing*
down all the desk lids. This reveals the group in various stages of sleep.

The group move to the back of the stage, except for **Father***, who is at the end of the table.*

> At noon, the shop experienced a momentary pause and relaxation: the hour of the afternoon siesta . . . the shop assistants abandoned themselves for a moment to the delights of yawning and turned somersaults on the bales of cloth. *The Dead Season*

Joseph *watches the shop inhabitants in a playful mood. The shop is sleeping.*

Joseph (*blows on his* **Father***'s head*)   Father.

The sound of birds flapping. **Father** *wakes momentarily.*

Father   Genus avium, bubus alba. (*He makes the hoot of an owl.*)

Joseph (*tries to imitate him, unsuccessfully. He runs to his* **Mother**.)   Mother. (*He finds an egg in her hair.*)

Mother (*wakes momentarily*)   . . . Egyptian cotton white lilac twenty-five pillow cases which I ordered from Warsaw and nobody ever knows if they're going to deliver them on a Thursday or a Friday. Ah, there you are!

Joseph *runs to the roll of cloth SL and touches it. He runs to the back of the shop and touches the coats there. The coats emit sounds of their previous owners. He smells* **Adela.** *She yawns and stretches in her slumber.*

Father (*runs to the back, still asleep*)   June, July, September . . . Where's August? I can't find August!

Theodore *runs to the front and back again. He and* **Leon** *come to the front and fall on the counter in front of* **Father***, who takes letters from his hand and pushes the* **Assistants** *towards* **Mother***.*

Father   Thank you.

Adela*'s unsuccessful cleaning of the counter is blocked by* **Mother***'s head.* **Leon** *and* **Theodore** *lift* **Mother***'s head for* **Adela** *to clean. The sound of* **Mother** *laughing. The* **Assistants** *lie on the counter again, holding their rolls of cloth.* **Adela** *goes back to the back wall.*

3 Father's beautiful shop

It was the age of electricity and mechanics and a whole swarm of
inventions was showered on the world by the resourcefulness of
human genius . . . in every house electric bells were installed.
The Comet

Joseph   Wake up . . . wake up. (*Bangs one of the desk lids.*)

Assistants *unroll two lengths of cloth, which hurtle downstage.*
Father *and* **Mother** *awake.* **Maria**, **Agatha**, **Emil** *and*
Charles *stand up like dummies* USL.

Father   The cloth, the cloth.

Mother   Yes indeed, the cloth.

Father   Who among the present generation of textile
merchants remembers the good traditions of their ancient
art? Who remembers, boys, that if you fold the cloth
according to the principles it will emit a sound like a
descending scale?

Mother   Like a descending scale

Father   At the touch of a finger, Theodore.

Mother   Not even a finger, Jacob.

Father   Not even a finger.

Mother   Not even a – boys, boys, open the shop !

Music from light entertainment radio of the era.

Assistants *leave the cloth and* **Father** *and run to the back wall.
They grab* **Adela** *and lift her on to the counter.* **Joseph** *joins in.*

Joseph   Adela, open the shop.

Adela *begins scrubbing the floor.* **Mother** *and* **Father** *continue a
long-running argument as they dance.* **Mother** *and the* **Assistants**
dress the dummies. **Joseph** *watches* **Adela** *from behind a coat.*
Father *climbs to his office on the back wall.* **Joseph** *rolls* **Maria**,
Emil, **Agatha** *and* **Charles** *out of the shop to become shoppers*
USL. **Leon** *and* **Theodore** *push a pole through* **Adela**'s *legs and*

carry her on it. **Father** *whistles at them. The shoppers are coming.*
They panic to find the door handle and bell. Coming to the shop, **Emil**
chatters to **Charles** *and* **Agatha** *about what they are going to buy.*

Emil   Veréis qué tienda tan meravillosa. La más moderna.
Os voy a enseñar los avances de la técnica, el futuro, un
timbre eléctrico, lo automático, con dinero se puede todo!
(*Indicates the* **Assistants**' *bell. Standing outside the shop he*
manages to get hold of the door handle, which the **Assistants** *have*
been annoyingly playing with.) Aha!

Emil, Charles *and* **Agatha** *sweep in, and stand DSR.*

Charles, Agatha, the mystery of electricity. It rings by itself.

Agatha   Really?

Charles   I don't believe it!

Emil   You will . . . brrrrrrr (*Makes sound of bell.*) . . .
Automático.

They sweep up to the counter.

Good morning!

Assistants   Djin Dobre!

Emil   Now listen . . . I have come with my friends to buy
. . . para comprar un timbro eléctrico.

Maria, *the little orange one, slips in front of* **Emil** *to try and buy*
something first.

Emil   Señorita, se ha colado usted . . .

Maria *takes no notice.*

Emil   Señorita, estaba yo primero . . .

Maria *continues to take no notice,* **Emil** *gives up temporarily.*

Here follows a whole number of **Maria** *attempting to communicate*
with **Joseph** *and show him her plate. The* **Assistants** *think*
Maria *wants to buy something and deliberately play games with her,*
seizing her plate and pretending to match it with all sorts of absurd

*objects, finishing with a real plate which they smash. She snatches back
her precious half plate and runs away. This is* **Emil**'s *chance to get
in. He takes it.*

Emil   Vamos aver por favor, despáchenme, que no tengo
toda la mañana. Good morning, now listen. Good Morning!

He finally has the attention of the **Assistants**.

Assistants   Djin Dobre!

Emil   Djin Dobre! . . . Herr Jacob?

Assistants (*turning to* **Mother**)   Herr Jacob?

Mother   Komm später.

Assistants   Komm später!

Emil   Well never mind, now listen. Yo lo que quiero es un
timbre eléctrico; 'The mystery of electricity, it rings by
itself.' (*He reads from the newspaper.*) 'El simbolo del progresso,
la téchnica y lo automático, aquí para mis amigos . . .'

Charles   We're hoping for a demonstration.

Agatha   Yes. And I would like to be the one to pay for it.
No, no I insist . . .

Here the **Assistants** *who have understood nothing, play a joke on*
Agatha *and give her a bone instead of the bell. The bone routine then
ensues. Being thrown back and forth until . . .*

Emil   Agatha! Charles, Charles, you explain, Charles,
Charles, they don't understand. Listen . . .

Charles   Yes, it's really very simple. All my friend is
asking for is . . .

Assistants   Capeluche?

They get out a couple of top hats. They start putting them on
Charles's *and* **Emil**'s *head. Confusion reigns. They speak
simultaneously.*

Charles No, no, no, listen, you didn't understand. I don't want a hat. I want . . . where is my hat . . . what? (*Hits himself over the head with a bone.*) Give me my hat, EMIL!!

Emil No, no, no, no, I don't want a capeluche. What I want is one of these. (*Indicates newspaper.*) No, no, what are you doing What . . . no . . . no . . . what . . . no . . . BASTA!! We'll try again! Now listen . . .

Passing in front of the counter as they change sides, he gets given the bone; he smells it and it makes him sneeze.

Emil Atchooo . . . (*Throws the bone away.*) Now listen . . . yo lo que quiero es un timbre eléctrico . . . An electric bell!

Charles Voilà!

Emil Se le da al botoncito, core por un circuito eléctrico galvanizado y prrrrrrrrr! Suena dentro de la casa, automático!

Assistants *shake a pair of fake castanets at him.*

Emil No, no, no, no. Es automatico. Que se le da al botoncito, core por un circuito electrico galvanizado y prrrrrrrrr! Atchoo!!!! (*Looks for handkerchief from* **Agatha** *and* **Charles**.) No tiene un handkerchief por favor? No? Enfin . . . Que se le da al botoncito, corre poor un circuito electrico galvanizado y prrrrrrrrr! Atchoo!!!!

This time the **Assistants** *have put his coat sleeve under his nose and* **Emil** *has had enough of their fooling around.*

Oiga! Pero, que me estan manchando el abrigo nuevo de mocos! Charles! Pero esto es disgusting; me están faltando al respecto. Que se la están buscando. Que yo se boxe, que yo se boxe, que la aprendí en Paris, que le doy, que le doy, que soy un campeón, hop, hop. What are you doing? You've ruined my new coat . . . Charles . . . Look . . . this is disgusting. I see . . . I see . . . you are looking for trouble!

Don't think I haven't noticed! Que se la están buscando.
Que yo se boxe, que la aprendí in Paris, que le doy, que.

Emil *and the* **Assistants** *start to pretend to fight. Chaos.*

> An electric bell is an ordinary mystification. The fabric of life can
> be found within the weave of a cloth. *The Comet*

Father (*whistles from his perch*)   Good heavens, Theodore,
Leon, I never knew we'd ordered so many eggs.

Emil   Hombre Jacob. At last. I have come here
tranquilamente y estos señores me están faltando al respeto.

Mother   And how can we help you?

Emil   Estoy buscando un timbre eléctrico.

Father   I'm sorry?

Emil   I would like an electric bell.

Father (*comes down on a rope from his perch*)   An electric
bell . . . Why?

Emil   Why? Why? Because I have to show my friends
exactly how it works . . . the principles of connection,
electricity . . .

Father (*asking for the newspaper*)   May I see? Look Joseph, an
electric bell.

Emil   An electric bell.

Father   An electric bell is of course a miracle of modern
science.

Emil   Is progress . . .

Father   But it is an ordinary mystification.

Emil   It is an ordinary mystifica ca ca como?

Father   Progress? Well some may call it that. It is not man
who has broken into the laboratory of Nature, but Nature
who uses man's ingenuity for her own purposes.

Mother   Jacob, he only wants to buy something.

Emil   Exactemente.

Father   I'm sorry. Some Indian silk perhaps . . . Egyptian cotton . . . A Royal tartan . . . a Persian cadar?

Emil   No, no, no, . . . yo no quiero un Persian cadar . . .

Father   No, you're right the pattern is too heavy. Allow us to show the pure white calaphony from Malabar?

Emil   No, no, no, yo no quiero un calaphony from Malabar. Hombre, yo lo que quiero es un timbre eléctrico . . . Que se le da al botoncito, core por un circuito eléctrico y prrrrrrrrr. Atchoo!!!! Es automático, es progreso, moderno.

Father *takes a handkerchief from his top pocket.*

Emil   Maravilioso . . . pero yo lo que quiero un electric bell . . . Botoncito . . . Circuito . . . prrrrrrrrr. Atchoo!!!! (*As he searches for a handkerchief.*) Perdón, qué tengo una alergia y no puedo hablar, perdón qué raro. Pero lo importante, es un timbre eléctrico. ¿Que hace Jacob?

Father *takes a handkerchief from his wig.* **Emil** *irritatedly snatches the handkerchief.*

Emil   Perfecto . . . Un electric bell . . . Botoncito . . . Circuito . . . prrrrrrrrr . . . Atchoo!!!! (*Underneath the action.*) Pero qué hace, qué me pica, qué dolor eléctrico rapido, Charles, Charles, una conexíon!

Father *does a magic trick.* **Emil** *shrieks and shakes as the hankerchief travels round his body.* **Charles** *removes it from his sock. General applause and amazement.*

Emil   Fantástico!

Father   An electric bell is of course a miracle of modern science, but the migration of forms is the essence of life. The fabric of life can be found within the weave of a cloth.

Emil   Cloth.

Charles/Agatha   Cloth . . .

Father   Allow us to show this with the calaphony from Malabar?

Emil   Hombre, it's not what I wanted, but if you insist . . .

Father   The true calaphony comes from the robes of the ritual dancers of Hipporabundia . . .

Emil   Hipporabundia . . .

Charles/Agatha   Hipporabundia . . .

Father   Now listen. (*He passes his hands over the cloth. It makes a ringing sound.*)

Emil (*genuinely surprised*)   An electric bell!

Charles   An electric bell.

Father   If you fold the cloth according to the principles it will emit a sound like a descending scale.

Mother   Gentlemen, my husband, a remarkable man in spite of everything, truly remarkable.

Father (*unfolds the cloth with the aid of the two* **Assistants**) This cloth pulsates with infinite possibilities that sends dull shivers through it. Indulgently acquiescent, pliable like a woman . . .

Joseph   Like a woman!

Father   It is a territory outside any law, a domain of beauty and godlike manipulation. Modern science however is transient and temporary.

The cloth begins to move. **Emil**, **Charles**, **Agatha** *and* **Maria** *move with it, apparently knocked off balance by its beauty. This rapidly leads to a dance. Behind the screen of the tablecloth the shop counter is being transformed into the dining room table.*

4   Family dinner

> We lived on Market Square, in one of those dark houses with
> empty blind looks, so difficult to distinguish one from the other.
> *Visitation*

The family sit round the table, in this order:

Charles   **Mother**   **Agatha**   *[empty chair]*

Joseph   **Emil**

Assistants *exit.* **Adela** *and* **Maria** *stand by the stove.*

Joseph *greets everyone at the table.*

Mother   Ah, Joseph! There you are!

Joseph   I'm sorry I'm late. Cousin Emil . . . (*He tries to kiss
his cousin.*)

Emil   Cheech la mano! Que ya eres un hombre!
Hipporabundia and Madagascar!

Agatha   Careful!

She puts **Joseph**'*s hands on her breasts. They embrace,* **Joseph** *a
little uncomfortably.*

Hasn't he grown!

Joseph *embraces his mother.* **Charles** *takes a letter out of*
Joseph'*s pocket.*

Charles   Love letters?

Emil   You're a man now.

Joseph *sits.*

Noise of birds flapping in the roof.

Everybody looks up. With the exception of **Joseph** *they all remain
immobile for the next scene.*

5   The maids

Maria was a woman who hired herself to housewives to scrub
floors. She was a small saffron-yellow woman, and it was with
saffron that she wiped the floors, the deal tables, the benches, and
the banisters which she had scrubbed in the homes of the poor.
August

Maria   Adela

Adela   Maria

Adela *and* **Maria**, *who is smoking a cigarette and clutching an
enormous book to her chest, walk from USR to the tap.* **Adela** *fills the
bucket with water.*

You know Maria, when I was a little girl we had no running
water.

Maria   No running water?

Adela   Water was precious.

Maria   Precious.

Adela   Yes, I was only allowed to wash myself once a week

Maria   Once a week?

Adela   Yes.

Maria   Once a week?

Adela   What?

Maria   You must have stunk, Adela.

Adela   Zigorette.

Maria   Adela, that's my cigarette.

Adela   You shouldn't smoke, Maria, it's very bad for your
health.

Maria   It's bad for your health.

Adela   No, your health . . .

Maria   Your health . . .

Adela/Maria   Your health . . . Your health . . . Your
health . . .

Adela *puts out the cigarette in the bucket of water.*

Maria   But Adela, you said water was precious.

Adela   I say many things, Maria . . . hurry up!

Maria *gives* **Adela** *her red shoes from the big book.*

Maria   But . . . Adela.

Adela   Maria, carry my boots.

Maria *puts* **Adela***'s boots inside the big book.* **Adela** *puts on her
red shoes.*

Maria   Yes . . . Adela . . .

Adela   Maria, what did I just say?

Maria   Carry my boots.

Adela   Yes!

Maria   But Adela . . .

Adela   Maria . . .

Maria   Yes?

Adela   Silence is golden.

They return to the stove.

6   The table of boredom

The days passed, the afternoons grew longer: there was nothing to
do in them. A yellow monotony, an elemental boredom. We were
inclined to underrate the value of Father's sovereign magic, which
saved us from the lethargy of empty days and nights.
Tailor's Dummies

Sound of birds flapping.

The cruet set flies in gracefully.

Mother   Ah! There you are!

Adela (*marches to the table with spoons and dishcloth*)   Oxtail soup.

Mother   Oxenswantzsuppe!

Charles   Wunderbar!

Emil   Maravilloso! Ostersoops!

Adela   Oxtail!

Emil   Oster . . . ?

Adela   OX!

Emil   Os . . . es lo que dico, Ostersoops . . . is my favourite dish. Every time I go to Paris I insist on having this magnificent soup, because I think it is a superb soup . . .

He becomes hypnotised by **Adela***'s onanistic cleaning of the cutlery beside him.* **Adela** *registers his sexual excitement, hits him in disgust and the plates tumble out on to the table. First two from* **Emil***, then* **Agatha***, then* **Mother** *and lastly* **Charles** *who for some unknown reason brings out a bottle instead of a plate. He rectifies this quickly with two more plates.*

Sound of violent bird flapping overhead.

Feathers fall from the ceiling.

Mother   Birds! Up in the attic with Father! At great expense of time and money, Father has imported from Hamburg and Holland and zoological stations in Africa . . .

Emil   Africa . . .

Charles/Agatha   Shhh!

Mother   Rare birds' eggs, which he has set up in the attic under enormous brood hens from Belgium.

Charles   La Belgique.

Emil   Belgica.

Adela   Belgian hens. (*She holds* **Joseph**'s *head and polishes a spoon on her breast.*) Yes but the point is, we eat later and later every day.

Mother   Adela . . .

Adela *leaves the table.*

Joseph *picks up the spoon that* **Adela** *was polishing and starts to kiss it. The rest of the table is slightly taken aback at this auto-eroticism. They laugh to cover their embarrassment.*

Mother   He's trying to hatch them.

Agatha   He's trying to hatch them.

Mother   Hatch them . . .

Agatha   Hatch them . . .

They laugh together. Then they sigh. All look gloomily out front. The clock begins to tick. **Agatha**'s *fan takes the rhythm of the clock.* **Emil** *notices* **Agatha**'s *fan.*

Emil   Joseph, did I ever tell you about my time in Africa . . . ? Well we were on safari in Uganda, Tanganika and Mozambique . . . Una tarde de verano muy calorosa. Qué calor, África. Cuando de pronto saliendo de la espesura se avalanzó sobre nosotros un rinoceronte. Yo se cómo son esos animales cuando se enrabietan, pero allí me quedé, haciéndole frente solo ante el peligro, los demás salieron por piernas, ha, ha, . . . Pero he aquí que un tigre, un elefante, un gorila, un hippopótamo . . . en fin manadas enteras de animales salvajes empezaron a venir; yo por supuesto, saqué mi rifle apunte y me puse a pegar tiros como un valiente y túe qué sabes que cuadro másh impresionante . . .

Emil *sees his own reflection in his cigarette case and gets distracted. He forgets completely that he is recounting an exciting story. He suddenly rediscovers his rapt audience.*

Oh, enfin . . . the whole adventure was very dangerous, very!

Mother   How very nice for you.

Agatha *laughs.*

The clock ticks. Boredom.

Charles *starts to fall asleep into his soup plate. As he hits the plate . . .*

Emil   Constantinopla!

Charles   Ah yes!

Boredom.

Now perhaps is the moment I might draw a parallel between Alexander the Great and my modest self. Alexander was susceptible to the aroma of countries. He felt as unfulfilled as I, he hungered after ever wider horizons and landscapes. There was no one who could point out his mistake. Not even Aristotle could understand him.

Father *enters from SR ladder.*

> My father, that incorrigible improvisor, that fencing master of the imagination led colourful and splendid counter-offensives of fantasy against the boredom that strangled the city. *Tailor's Dummies*

Father   The birds!

All   Jacob!

Father   Joseph, you should see the birds, the curlews have come back and the peacocks . . . eggs the colour of dreams.

Joseph   Father.

Mother   Ah Jacob, there you are!

Father   By the way Hettie, you were right, we are missing a month . . .

Mother   No, it's not missing.

Father   June, July . . . here's September, but I can't find August.

Adela *enters with soup and stands waiting to serve.*

Father (*sees* **Charles**)   I am sorry. I am concerned with this section of space which you are filling.

Charles *goes to the other end of the table and sits on the chair offered to him by* **Adela**. *She is still waiting to serve the soup.* **Father** *sits. He brings out a bird's egg.*

Father   Matter is in a state of constant fermentation. It never holds the same shape for very long. Am I to conceal from you . . .

Mother   Oh, please will somebody shut him up.

Everybody looks at **Adela** *in expectation.*

Father   No Hettie please, I must tell this story . . .

Adela *advances towards* **Father**.

Father   Adela, please.

She tickles him until he can bear it no longer. He is silent. **Adela** *has won their first battle. She raises her finger at him in warning and goes back to serve the soup. She stirs the pot of soup gently, as* **Father** *watches in fascination. She suddenly notices that* **Emil** *is getting an erotic charge off this motion. She slaps some soup in his plate, to put an end to it. She serves* **Charles**, *who is also excited by the way in which she does it. Then she goes to* **Mother**.

Mother   Und ein kleines bisschen mehr.

Adela/Mother   And a little bit more . . .

Adela *serves* **Agatha**.

Agatha   And a little bit more . . .

She doesn't get any more. **Adela** *serves* **Father** *and* **Joseph**. **Joseph** *is holding the egg.*

Adela   Joseph, stop playing with the egg, we are eating now.

Father   Very remarkable, very remarkable indeed.

Mother   Thank you Adela. Well, you must all be completely exhausted.

Charles *and* **Emil** *agree. Everyone settles down to eat.*

Father (*excitedly pushes his soup away*)   Am I to conceal from you . . .

Adela   Herr Jacob we are eating now.

Father   No, I must tell you this story . . . Adela please.

Adela *puts* **Father***'s soup back in front of him. He pushes it away. Repeat five times.*

Adela (*waves a spoon at him*)   No!

Everyone watches, electrified, as – very slowly – **Father** *capitulates and takes a mouthful of soup.*

Father   Wunderbar soup Adela, wunderbar.

Adela   Bon appétit! (*Exits.*)

The meal begins. Everyone chatters loudly. **Father** *checks that* **Adela** *is no longer in the vicinity.*

Father   Am I to conceal from you . . . Emil, Charles, listen. (*He is unable to attract anybody's attention.*)

Mother *is talking to* **Agatha**. **Charles** *is listening to* **Emil**.

Father *hatches a plan. He creeps behind* **Charles** *and, while* **Charles** *is not looking, switches the cigar round, so that the lit end now faces* **Charles***'s mouth.* **Father** *nips back to his chair and awaits the result.* **Charles** *cries out in pain.*

Mother   Jacob!

Father (*takes his opportunity*)   Am I to conceal from you that my own brother, as a result of a long and incurable illness, has been gradually transformed into a bundle of rubber tubing?

Adela *returns to the table.*

Father   Can there be anything sadder than a human being changed into the rubber tube of an enema? What a disappointment for his parents. And yet the faithful love of my cousin, who used to carry him day and night on a cushion . . .

Mother   Adela!

Adela *lifts her fingers, threatening to start tickling* **Father** *again, who begins laughing at the merest suggestion.*

Father   And yet the faithful love of my cousin . . . the faithful love . . . No, no, please stop . . .

His laughing becomes painful. **Adela** *does not stop the torture.*

We need the privilege of creation . . . we need creative delights . . .

In one gesture, **Adela** *cuts off his laughter. With a second gesture, he reacts as if smacked round the face. With* **Adela***'s third gesture (as if she were throwing something into the pot), he collapses on to his chair like a sack of potatoes. He is humiliated.*

> Adela's complexion, under the influence of the springward gravitation of the moon, became younger, acquired milky reflexes, opaline shades and the glaze of enamel. She now had the whip hand . . . *The Comet*

All begin laughing and chattering again to cover their embarrassment. **Joseph** *touches* **Father** *in sympathy.*

Father (*stands up*)   Matter doesn't make jokes. It is always full of the tragically serious.

As he begins this, the table falls silent but appears to be continuing its chatter. He sits down again. The voices of everyone at the table return. He stands again.

You may laugh, but in the wink of an eye . . .

He becomes aware that again the table has fallen silent, while appearing to continue their chatter. He is surprised, then delighted. He tries it two or three times – standing and sitting.

Matter is in a state of constant fermentation. Matter can change in an instant, Joseph. (*He takes out his magnifying glass and makes* **Joseph** *look at the table through it.*) In the wink of an eye we may no longer be who we think we are.

Emil, **Charles**, **Agatha**, **Mother**, **Maria**, **Adela**, **Leon** *and* **Theodore** *turn into birds.*

Father (*walks on to the table*)   Genus Avium . . .

The people, now birds, respond with a chorus of bird calls.

Joseph   Oh Father . . . your birds, Father.

A chorus of bird calls.

Father   Very remarkable, very remarkable indeed. This is ibis ibis, the Spanish stork. (*He points out* **Emil** *and gets down off the table.*)

Joseph   May I feed them?

Father   Of course you can feed them, Joseph. Here we have the wrens . . . (*He points out* **Adela** *and* **Maria**.)

Joseph   From England!

Father   Trogladytes, trogladytes, trogladytes . . .

Joseph (*points out* **Charles**)   Columba aquatica.

Father   Not quite Joseph, columba aquatrix.

Joseph (*points at* **Leon** *on the wall*)   This is cuccus solitarius.

Father (*points at* **Theodore** *on the table*)   And this is cuccus lacteus, Joseph, and here we have a . . . (*Looks at* **Agatha**.)

Joseph   A peacock!

Father   And here is a broody hen . . . (*Looks at* **Mother**.)

The birds chorus to a climaxing response. **Joseph** *takes a book and it begins to flap and fly like a bird.*

Joseph   Oh Father . . . your birds, Father.

Behind his back, in three movements, the scene dissolves back to the table.

Adela (*takes* **Joseph** *by the ear and makes him sit down*)   Joseph . . . we are eating now!

Father   Very remarkable . . .

Adela (*in warning, raising her finger*)   Herr Jacob!

Father *defies her and calls to his birds with the sound of a cuckoo.* **Adela** *raises her ladle. As she does so a piece of birdshit falls, loudly, on to the cloth. Outrage from everyone.*

Father   Theodore, Leon, this is a very remarkable stool . . . It's ibis ibis the Spanish stork!

Adela   That is the limit.

Mother   Adela, please . . .

Adela   I do not believe it, birdshit on the tablecloth . . .

Mother   I can see what it is.

Adela   No! I was not employed here to clean up birdshit . . .

Mother   I know.

Adela   Herr Jacob is getting wilder and wilder every day, now he has a bird hospital up in the attic.

Father *hides behind his ledger.*

Mother   Adela, please we'll talk . . .

Adela   No! Just look at the new tablecloth, it's completely ruined . . . and it stinks!

Mother   Adela, you are a wonderful girl.

All   Yes, wonderful . . .

Mother   Wonderful in every way, don't think of leaving us. Jacob, you must apologise, we have a problem.

Father   Yes, you're right, we do have a problem, we're missing a month.

Mother   What do you mean we're missing a month?

Father   I can't account for the seasons. June, July, here's September . . . but I can't find August.

Mother It's on the calico where you left it.

Father   No I couldn't have mislaid it, you must have mislaid it.

Mother   Apologise!

Father   Adela . . .

Mother   Apologise!

Father   August, August, August . . .

Mother   That's enough! Put it with the other months.

Adela   Yes!

Mother *takes the ledger and gives it to* **Adela**. **Father** *snatches it back as she walks past.*

Adela   Herr Jacob, bring me that month!

Father   Not until you bring me August . . .

Adela   Bring it to me . . .

Father   August . . .

Adela   Bring it here . . .

Father   August . . .

Adela   Right that's it. Give it here.

The ledger is snatched by **Mother**, *passed from* **Assistant** *to* **Assistant** *and back to* **Father**. **Adela** *promptly takes it away again. The ledger takes on a life of its own, responding to* **Father**'s *transformational abilities. The ledger flies out of* **Adela**'s *hands, through the* **Assistants**, *down the table, making a big circle, ending with* **Joseph** *who returns it to* **Father**. *With everyone hanging on,* *the ledger sways to and fro, until the group is catapulted towards ledgers placed around the room.* **Adela** *is the only one unaffected. In disgust, she picks up her bucket and, with* **Maria***, goes to the tap. The ledgers now have control of everyone. They fly DSC back up to* **Father***, round the table, eventually ending – with the music – when* **Emil** *sits on his chair and the books fall on top of him.* **Adela** *bangs down her bucket at the tap. All watch her as she returns angrily to the stove.*

7   August

The untidy, feminine ripeness of August had expanded into enormous, impenetrable clumps of burdocks . . . with their luxurient tongues of fleshy greenery . . . a tangled thicket of grasses, weeds and thistles crackled in the fire of the afternoon. The sleeping garden was resonant with flies. *August*

Adela *bangs bucket beside the stove. With a great show of patience she opens the stove and takes out a ledger. She throws it on the table in front of the assembled company.*

Adela   August!

Father   Adela . . . (*Tries to grab the ledger.*)

Adela   Don't touch it!

Father *tries again.*

Adela   Hands off!

Joseph (*takes the book. He kisses it. He touches it with his forehead. He gives it to* **Mother***.*)   August. (*He begins to open the book.*)

Mother   Ah, August . . .

Everyone looks into the book.

Mother (*continues to open the book. She stands on her chair.*)   The endless holidays . . .

Everyone looks out front as if they can see the endless holidays.
Mother *steps on to the table. The chairs move apart mirroring the opening pages. The family group help* **Mother** *over the table.*

Days and days and days full of the sweet melting pulp of golden pears. And the ripe morello cherries that smelled so much better than they tasted. The golden squares of sunlight falling on a wooden floor. A distant chord played on a piano over and over.

She has come down the other side of the table towards the audience. **Joseph** *is sitting on* **Leon**'s *shoulders.* **Emil** *and* **Theodore** *are holding the books as if they were a set of bannisters.*

And I would walk with Joseph in Market Square. It was completely empty, you see, nobody there. And yes, yes . . . I had had a little wine . . .

The books collapse, changing from a banister into a small seat for **Agatha**. *Everyone looks towards* **Adela** *at the tap.* **Adela** *turns towards them and takes off her dress, revealing pink beneath the green.*

Ah, there you are.

Leon *and* **Theodore** *lift up the tablecloth over the heads of the seated group and place it in front of them on the ground, like a picnic napkin.* **Mother** *sits down behind it with* **Emil**, **Charles** *and* **Agatha**, *DSC.* **Maria** *puts a long parasol into a hole on the table.* **Adela** *advances towards the group, leaving her shoes on the DSL corner of the cloth. She kicks* **Theodore** *languidly out of the way. She pours* **Mother** *some raspberry syrup. It is hot. Adela sits on the cloth in front of them, with* **Maria**. **Father** *sits just behind everyone, up on the table. He looks at* **Adela**.

Father   How delightful and happy is the form of existence which you ladies have chosen. How beautiful and simple is the truth which is revealed by your lives. If forgetting the respect due to the Creator I were to attempt criticism of creation, I would say less matter more form. What a relief it would be for the world to lose some of its contents, just some of its contents.

A buzzing fly is swatted on the tablecloth by **Theodore**.

Agatha   Joseph, do you remember, when we were children we used to play together. (*She stands up, taking*

Joseph *by the hand towards the tap.*) On Stryska Street, there is a pharmacy and in the window a huge jar of raspberry juice which they claimed could cure all summer ills. (*She tries to get some raspberry syrup out of the tap. Nothing emerges.*)

Joseph *escapes to the group. He waves* **Emil**'s *hand. Waving* **Emil**'s *hand reminds* **Emil** *of the heat.*

Emil   Qué calor! Como en África. This provincial climate is known by the experts as a Chinese summer in *China* of course . . . China . . . China . . . China . . .

(*He is unable to pronounce the word China without his voice cracking.* **Charles** *helps by tuning him to his banjo. This makes* **Emil** *begin to sing.*) China, thank you, China it is too long . . . (*Realises he is singing and stops in embarrassment.*) Hem . . . far too long. In Alaska, for example, the summer is only this long, and then it's finished.

Charles   Do you know why animals have horns? It is because they have such incredible imaginations. Their fantasies, unlike ours, emerge into the air above their heads and take on weird unpredictable shapes . . . A sort of *idée fixe*.

Theodore *and* **Leon** *play with the iron on the cloth.* **Maria** *and* **Adela** *play with the cutlery. We focus on* **Joseph**. *He points* **Charles**' *finger at* **Emil**'s *hair.*

Charles   Excuse me.

Emil   Yes?

Charles   Is that a real wig?

Emil   And that. (*Pushes back* **Charles**'s *hat.*) Is that a real bald patch?

Mother, **Agatha** *and* **Emil** *roar with laughter.* **Emil** *throws his head back in laughter and his wig falls off. He quickly puts it back on and stands patting* **Mother**'s *hand, absolutely mortified.* **Joseph** *sees* **Adela**'s *shoes and goes and lays his head beside them on the floor. He takes one and puts it, heel down, on his face.* **Adela** *comes to*

retrieve it. The **Assistants** *begin to get lascivious with* **Adela**.
Father *watches from the table.*

Father   Do you understand the horrible cynicism of this
symbol on a woman's foot, Joseph? Of her licentious walk
on such elaborate heels, you do not understand. It's God's
fault, God's to blame . . . For too long we have lived under
the terror of the matchless perfection of the Creator. We
don't wish to compete with him. We have no ambition to
emulate him. We wish to be creators in our own lower
sphere; we want to have the privilege of creation, we want
creative delights, we want, in one word, godliness.

> My father, exhausted by the heat . . . shook himself violently,
> buzzed, and rose in fright before our eyes, transformed into a
> monstrous, hairy steel blue horsefly . . . we recognised that my
> father's transformation was a symbol of an inner protest, a violent
> and desperate demonstration of suffering. *The Dead Season*

Father, *infuriated, leaps down from the table.*

The sound of flies buzzing.

Everyone tries to swat the swarm of flies which has descended on them.
Adela *DSL holding the fly swat, grabs one fly.*

Buzzing stops.

*Silence. Everyone stops for a moment of complete immobility. She
releases the fly.*

The buzzing re-starts.

Father *begins to turn into a fly. He buzzes round the* **Assistants**
and **Adela**, *then* **Charles** *and* **Agatha** *and* **Emil**. *The*
Assistants *take the ends of the tablecloth and it is caught up round*
Father's *waist. He comes to DSC where he stands transfixed and
buzzing furiously.* **Maria**, *unseen, makes his insect antennae with
two forks above his head.* **Father** *releases himself from the cloth.*
Joseph *follows the cloth as it is draped back over the table.* **Adela**
*pursues a fly round the table in front of the diners, who push their
chairs back to give her room. She kills the fly with her fly swatter.*
Father *collapses DSC.*

8   The killing of the birds

> One day, during spring cleaning, Adela suddenly appeared in
> Father's bird kingdom .... A fiendish cloud of feathers and wings
> arose screaming, and Adela, like a furious maenad protected by
> the whirlwind of her thyrsus, danced the dance of destruction ...
> A moment later, my father came downstairs – a broken man, an
> exiled king who had lost his throne and his kingdom. *Birds*

Mother   Really, Jacob, having fallen into this lamentable
condition why have you not the strength of spirit or dignity
to bear it without complaint?

Leon *and* **Theodore** *pick up* **Father** *from the floor and replace
him on his chair.* **Adela** *takes the fly and drops it in the stove. All give
one last death-throe buzz.*

Father   Matter! (*He goes to the stove.*) We should weep when
we see the misery of that violated matter. (*He goes to the table,
clutching a pile of plates.*) Matter never makes jokes. Even this
plate has infinite fertility. In the depths of this clay indistinct
smiles are shaped, attempts at form appear . . .

Adela *takes the plate away from him.*

Father (*picks up a book*)   Do you understand the mystery of
these sheaves, these arabesques of Indian ink? . . .

Adela *takes the book from him. Birdshit falls on* **Charles** *twice.*
Emil *laughs and shit falls on him. As he complains, mouth open,
looking up, shit falls in his mouth. Soon it is raining birdshit.* **Father**
and **Joseph** *stand SR, watching. The others find umbrellas and try
to protect themselves, appalled.*

Adela (*grabs* **Father**'s *egg*)   Enough is enough! (*She takes the
egg from* **Father** *and breaks it into a plate.*) I have had it up to
here! (*She storms DSL to the tap.*)

Father (*mournfully holding up the running egg yolk*)   I knew a
certain sea-captain who had in his cabin a lamp made by
Malayan embalmers from the body of his murdered
mistress.

In the stunned silence, **Mother** *speechlessly gropes for comfort, reason and laments her lot. Finally, she points in the direction of the attic and . . .*

Mother   These birds, these eggs Jacob, they're dreams, worthless dreams. Adela!

Adela   Frau Jacob.

Mother   They're in the attic!

Everyone points in the direction of the attic. **Adela** *strides towards her appointed task – to clear the attic of the birds.* **Adela** *climbs the ladder SR.*

Joseph   Mother, what are you doing?

While **Joseph** *is arguing with his family,* **Father** *attempts to follow* **Adela***. He is held back by the* **Assistants***. The stage darkens. The family become the birds in the attic.* **Father** *and* **Adela** *re-emerge USR, as if they have climbed to the top of the house.* **Joseph** *watches from DSR in horror.* **Adela** *and* **Father** *approach the table and hide behind it.* **Adela** *opens a desk lid. Light pours out. She is in the attic. She confronts the birds. The birds flap and squawk. Three times she tries to get rid of them. When they run from their position at the table USL, they trace a huge circle round the table to DSL.* **Adela** *picks up a broom and chases the birds until they gather DSL.*

Adela (*USR*)   Out!

She charges them and they fly in terror. **Father** *becomes a condor on the desks. The umbrellas become his flapping wings behind him.* **Adela** *charges the condor and kills it with her broom.*

9   Tango

Lifting up with ease Adela's slim shoe, he spoke as if seduced by the lustrous eloquence of that empty shell of patent leather. 'Do you understand the horrible cynicism of this symbol on a woman's foot, the provocation of her licentious walk on such elaborate heels?' . . . *The Age of Genius*

Joseph   Adela . . .

The bird collapses.

Joseph   Adela . . .

The table disintegrates. **Joseph** *runs through it as the desks reassemble into the classroom. He is prevented from reaching* **Adela** *by the swinging desks. The class re-emerges, seated at their desks.* **Adela** *sweeps* **Father** / *the dying condor wrapped in the cloth out through DSR doors.* **Father** *crawls like a cockroach.*

Adela (*sings*)
   All the birdies they are here
   All the birdies so dear
   Blackbird, thrush, finch and crow
   Sitting pretty in a row
   All the birdies they are set free
   Joyful blessed and happy

She returns to her desk.

Joseph (*goes to her angrily*)   Adela! (*He seizes her arm as if he will hit her.*)

Joseph   Adela . . . Adela!

She takes a glass and a spoon from her desk and gives them to him.

Adela   Joseph . . .

From out of his top pocket, she takes a letter. He tries to seize it back. She runs across the room, returning only the envelope. She reads.

'Dear Sir,
I need a friend. I need the closeness of a kindred spirit. I long for some outside affirmation of the inner world whose existence I cherish. I need a partner for voyages of discovery. One person becomes reality when reflected in two pairs of eyes.

Emil *beats the rhythm of the tango with his pair of scissors.*

'My world has been waiting for this twosome, as it were. What was once a closed tight place with no further prospects now begins to ripen into colours in the distance, burst open and reveal its depths.' (*She throws away the letter.*)

Joseph *is utterly bewitched by her. The rest of the cast have collected their musical instruments. They play the beat of the tango.* **Leon** *emerges with his violin. He is dressed in black. The tango begins.* **Joseph** *and* **Adela** *dance. He caresses her foot. He crawls behind her heel as she walks towards the tap. He kneels in front of her. She fills his glass from the tap. What emerges is milk. She holds him to her breast and feeds him the milk with a spoon. She joins the group playing the tango, all looking at him.* **Joseph** *turns to face them. The music stops.*

Joseph   Why are you doing this? Where is Father?

The band go crazy with a cacophonous din, laughing and playing.

No!

He throws the milk away. The figures around him fall to the ground, taking the rhythm of the wind in their bodies and still holding their instruments. Only **Leon** *continues to play the violin, like the figure of Death.* **Joseph** *rushes past him looking up at the back wall where* **Father** *sat in the shop.*

Father, Father.

Leon *plays a final note on his violin. The tap begins to run of its own accord. Everyone looks at it.* **Adela** *goes to turn it off. As she gets back to her desk,* **Joseph** *seizes her by the arm.*

Adela, where is Father? Adela, please, tell me where is Father?

Agatha *hands* **Joseph** *a book.*

Charles   Page twenty-two.

All
'Wer reitet so spät durch Nacht und Wind?
Es ist der Vater' . . .

Joseph   . . . Father.

All

. . . 'mit seinem Kind.
Er hat den Knaben wohl in dem Arm' . . .

Joseph   Mother, Mother, where are you going? Where is
Father?

Joseph *runs USC to where* **Mother** *sits. She is putting on her hat
and coat and gloves.*

Mother   Joseph, I had to get rid of them. They were very
noisy and dirty.

All

'Wer reitet so spät durch Nacht und Wind?
Es ist der Vater' . . .

Joseph   Where is Father? Mother, I'm asking you. What
have you done with Father?

Part Three: The Republic of Dreams

1   The branch line of time

> The train, which ran only once a week on that forgotten branch
> line, carried no more than a few passengers. Never before had I
> seen such archaic coaches . . . they exuded an air of strange and
> frightening neglect . . . *Conductor where are you? Sanatorium under
> the Sign of the Hourglass*

Joseph *bangs the lid of* **Mother***'s desk in fury. Again, as in a
nightmare – as if propelled by the violence of his action – the class hurl
themselves at the floor as if thrown by an invisible hand.*

All

> Wer reitet so spät . . .
> Wer reitet so spät . . .
> Wer reitet so spät . . .

*The class rise and fall with the words, gradually crawling DSC.
Confused,* **Joseph** *comes between them, trying to lift them.*
Theodore *gives him a suitcase. The class reassemble DSC as a
train, sitting on their chairs which they have brought with them. Their
words form the rhythm of the train moving. This rhythm continues
underneath the whole of the next scene.*

All

> Wer reitet so spät . . .
> Wer reitet so spät . . .
> Wer reitet so spät . . .

The group move as if on a rattling 1930s train. **Joseph** *clutches his
suitcase. For some reason, he is wearing* **Charles***'s hat.* **Charles**
irritably takes it back. They are now sitting in this order:

Maria	**Theodore**		**Charles**	**Agatha**
Mother	**Adela**		**Emil**	**Joseph**

Joseph   Mother! Mother!

Leon, *still dressed in black as the figure of Death, appears upstage of them as the ticket collector.*

Leon   Billets!!

Joseph   Mother. Where are we going, Mother?

Mother   Be quiet, Joseph, we're nearly there.

Leon   Bitte! Billets!!

Emil (*pointing to* **Joseph**'*s suitcase*)   Luggage! Luggage!

Joseph *tries to put his suitcase up on the rack. Everyone stands up to help. They form the wall of a corridor upstage of the chairs.*

Joseph   Mother! Mother!

Charles   Don't push!

The scream of train brakes.

The group hurtle upstage into the darkness. **Joseph**'*s suitcase is flung back at him as the train stops.*

2   The sanatorium

In the hallway of the many windowed hotel that advertised itself
as the sanatorium, there was semi-darkness and a solemn silence.
Dr Gotard was standing in the middle of the room to receive me.
'None of our patients know or can guess that the whole secret of
the operation is that we have put back the clock. Here your
father's death, the death that has already struck him in your
country, has not occurred yet . . .' *Sanatorium under the Sign of the
Hourglass*

Joseph *finds himself in somewhere completely new.* **Leon** *is
slumped over the DSR desk.* **Theodore** *sleeps on the USC desk.
Otherwise the room is empty.*

Joseph (*to* **Theodore**)   Excuse me.

Silence.

(*To* **Leon**.)   Excuse me . . .

Leon   Maid!

Joseph   Excuse me . . . I am looking for my father.

Leon   Maid!

Agatha *appears from USL doors, dressed as a nurse. She rearranges the desks on SL to form a bed.*

Joseph   Excuse me.

Agatha   Ssshh!

Joseph   I am looking for my father.

Agatha (*lays out a sheet on the bed*)   Ssshh! Everyone is asleep now.

Joseph   Asleep? During the day?

Agatha   All the time. It's always night here. Perhaps you could wait in the restaurant. (*She crosses to go out of DSR doors.*) When the doctor wakes up, I'll let him know you're here. (*She exits, laughing DSR.*)

Joseph *follows her.* **Leon** *suddenly sits up, frightening* **Joseph**. **Leon** *is still dressed in black as the figure of Death.*

Leon   We received your telegram. Are you well?

Joseph Is my father still alive?

Leon   Of course. Within certain limits. In your country, your father is dead, but here he is very much alive. Here we turn back the clock. Go straight through. It's the first door. The first door!

Joseph *advances DSR.* **Leon** *exits USL.*

Father (*appears on the back wall*)   The six days of Creation were divine and bright. But on the seventh day, God broke down.

Joseph   Father!

Father   How good of you to come . . .

Enter everyone, except for **Mother**, *as a group. They gaze at* **Joseph**.

. . . but why did you bring so many? So many . . . so many . . . so many?

Maria *comes between* **Father** *and* **Joseph**. *Laughing, she pushes him DSR. The rest of the group rush* **Father** *to the bed DSL.*

Maria (*to* **Joseph**)   I think he'll recognise you.

Father   He felt an unknown texture beneath his fingers and, frightened, withdrew from the world. (*He gets into bed behind a sheet held by* **Adela** *and* **Agatha**.)

Maria *runs in front of the bed and presents* **Father**.

Maria   Well?

Maria, *singing a little nursery song, suddenly whips out her half a plate and reveals herself as the lover from the beginning of the play.* **Joseph** *is confused. As he looks for his half,* **Leon**, **Theodore** *and* **Maria** *laugh at him and disappear into the darkness.*

Joseph   Hey! Hey!

Adela   Joseph!

Joseph   Adela!

Adela   What are you doing out of bed?

Father   No, don't go, please don't go.

Joseph *is about to get into bed when he notices a light coming out of the DSR doors. They swing open.*

Mother   Ah, Joseph, there you are.

Joseph   Mother!

> My father was slowly failing, wilting before our eyes. Hunched among the enormous pillows, his grey hair standing wildly on end, he talked to himself in undertones. It seemed as if his personality had split into a number of opposing and quarrelling selves; he argued loudly with himself, persuading forcibly and passionately, pleading and begging. *Visitation*

Father (*to* **Adela**)   I see you've polished your shoes.

Joseph *gets into bed with* **Father** *who is continuing his discussion with himself.* **Adela** *gives* **Father** *a glass of medicine, which is apparently not to his liking.*

Father   No, no, no, there is no dead matter. Lifelessness is only a disguise . . . I can't account for the seasons. Oh, Jacob, Jacob, Jacob . . . What? Yes? Yes? (*To* **Joseph**.) A boy in a million, a ministering angel. You must agree, gentlemen, he is a charmer. We have lived too long under the natural perfection of the Creator. Is that a smoking jacket? There is nothing to be done about this plague of dogs for example. (*Pointing.*) Look! The anarchist Luccheni . . . (*Pointing in another direction.*) Draga . . . The hope and pride of his ancient family ruined by the unfortunate habit of masturbation. Well, we need the privilege of creation, we want creative delights, we want, in one word, godliness . . .

Joseph   Father –

Father   Godliness!! (*He disappears under the sheets.*)

Joseph   Mother, where am I? What's happening here?

Mother   Ah, Joseph, now don't be frightened – it's only the wind. (*She comforts* **Joseph**.)
Wer reitet so spät durch Nacht und Wind?
Es ist der Vater mit seinem Kind.
Er hat den Knaben wohl in dem Arm
Er fasst ihn sicher er halt ihn warm,

Father (*reappears from under the sheets*)   Look after the shop, Joseph. Look to the shop. Ah, what a relief it would be for the world to lose some of its contents . . . just some of its contents . . .

Mother
Mein Sohn, was birgst du so bang dein Gesicht
Siehst, Vater, du den Erlkönig nicht
Den Erlenkönig mit Kron und Schweif?
Mein Sohn, es ist ein Nebelstreif.

Joseph *suddenly whips back the sheet. Instead of* **Father**'s *head, there is now* **Charles**'s. **Joseph** *leaps out of bed and stands before them all, confronting his* **Mother**.

    O Vater, O Vater, und hörest du nicht
    Was Erlenkönig mir leise verspricht?

Joseph   Mother –

Mother
    Sei ruhig, bleibe ruhig, mein Kind
    In durren Blättern sauselt der Wind.

She whips off the sheet revealing a pair of wooden dummy legs. **Emil** *puts them upright.*

There he is! He's a little thinner to be sure . . .

Theodore *and* **Leon** *appear above the legs with a set of dummy arms.* **Charles** *presents a dummy head of* **Father** *above this grotesquely assembled lifesize marionette which reminds us of* **Father**.

. . . but he's well on the way to recovery.

Emil   He's off his head!

Everybody laughs viciously. The group steps the dummy towards **Joseph**. *He runs round the class, the dummy pursuing him, until it dances in front of him DSC.*

Joseph   Stop it! (*He starts to wrestle with the dummy. It disintegrates in front of him. To* **Adela** *who has the legs.*) Get rid of it!

He watches in horror as **Adela** *is given a saw by* **Leon** *and she starts to saw the legs into small bits. As the legs are sawn, so* **Joseph**'s *legs seem to collapse themselves.*

Oh Mother!

Mother
    Ich liebe dich, mich reizt deine schone Gestalt
    Und bist du nicht willig, so brauch ich Gewalt
    O Vater, O Vater, jetzt fasst er mich an!
    Erlkönig hat mir ein Leids getan!

Dem Vater grausets, er reitet geschwind,
Er halt in Armen das achzende Kind
Erreicht den Hof mit Mühe und Not
In seinem Armen das Kind war tot.

Adela *finishes sawing through the first leg. The wood falls to the floor.*

Joseph   Dead! Mother! Father is dead!

My mother rushed in, frightened and enfolded my screams with
her arms, wanting to stifle them like flames and choke them in the
warmth of her love. She closed my mouth with hers and screamed
together with me. *The Age of Genius*

Mother   Don't torture me. Your father's away on a
business trip. He leaves very early in the morning and
comes back very late at night.

Joseph   Mother the shop! We must look after the shop!
(*He hurls* **Mother** *on to a desk.*) The shop!

*He violently creates the counter of the shop by straightening the desks
behind which the rest of the characters are sheltering. He appears to
pick up the entire line of desks by himself and they crash down in the
position of the original shop counter.*

3   The empty shop

I had a hidden resentment against my mother for the ease with
which she had recovered from Father's death. She had never
loved him, I thought . . . *Cockroaches*

Joseph'*s growing sense of desperation in this scene is not only about
an attempt to reverse time and refind his childhood but also a sense of
foreboding about the future. In the repetition of the gestures, he not only
expresses his anger and hurt at the disappearance of his father and by
extension his past, but also is attempting in some way to hold up time.*

Joseph (*bangs shut the desk lids*)   The shop! (*He forces*
Theodore *to ring the bell.*) Come in!

Charles   Good morning.

Emil   Good morning?

Agatha   Yes.

Joseph   Open the shop!

Assistants   Djin dobre.

Joseph *dances with* **Mother**. *The* **Assistants** *take off her coat. The taking off turns into a routine, which doesn't work.* **Mother** *stands on the counter. As in the first shop,* **Charles**, **Agatha** *and* **Emil** *appear as shoppers.*

Joseph   Open the shop.

The routine of coming into the shop with **Theodore** *ringing the bell,* **Leon** *opening the door with the door handle, the shoppers crossing from DSL to DSR, briefly watching* **Adela** *sawing* **Father**'s *legs (which she does continuously through this scene) and then stopping at DSL corner of the counter to ask* **Mother** *and the* **Assistants** *if they can buy something is a physical journey which is repeated almost exactly all three times. When the shoppers arrive in position,* **Mother** *raises her hand.*

Mother   And how can we help you?

Emil   Herr Jacob?

Mother   Herr Jacob?

Everyone momentarily looks at the remains of the marionette which **Adela** *is sawing up.*

Emil   I'd like a Royal tartan, please.

Assistants, *extremely rapidly, look in the desks. There is nothing there.*

Mother   I'm so sorry, we have nothing left.

Assistants   Niet material!

Another block of wood drops from **Adela**'s *saw.*

Joseph   No . . . !

Maria *throws the ledger on the floor.*

Mother the shop! It is wrong! Do it again.

He throws the shoppers out, cruelly throws his **Mother** *out and makes them do the whole routine again. This time it is a little shorter. All the figures are a little more delapidated. No one understands why they are being forced to do this.*

Joseph   Come in, come in . . .!

The bell rings. The shoppers enter. They end up in the same position at the DSL end of the counter.

Mother (*raises her hand*)   And how can we help you?

All momentarily glance once more at **Father** *being chopped up.*

Emil   I'd like a Persian cadar please.

Assistants, *extremely rapidly, look in the desks. There is nothing there.*

Mother   I'm so sorry, we have nothing left.

Assistants   Niet material!

Another block of wood drops from **Adela**'s *saw.*

Joseph   No!

Maria *throws the ledger on the floor.*

Joseph   Do it again! Again! Do it again!

Mother   Joseph.

Joseph   Mother! Come in, come in . . . ! (*He swings his* **Mother** *around and throws her against the counter.*)

The bell rings. The shoppers enter. They end up in the same position at the DSL end of the counter.

Mother (*raises her hand, sobbing*)   And how can we help you?

All momentarily glance once more at **Father** *being chopped up.*

Emil   I'd like a Royal tartan, a Persian cadar, an electric bell –

Charles   The calaphony –

Emil   The calaphony from Malabar.

Assistants, *extremely rapidly, look in the desks. There is nothing there.*

Mother   I'm so very sorry, but we have absolutely nothing left.

Assistants   Niet material!

Joseph   No!

Joseph *swings* **Mother** *around. She begins to turn on the spot. Everybody is turning as at the end of a nightmare.* **Mother** *crashes to the floor. The sound of a door-slam. A final block of wood falls from* **Adela***'s saw. She picks up all the wood, puts it on her tray and goes USR to the stove. She loads the stove with wood. Takes out a match and lights it. She slams the top of the stove.*

4   The landau – Mother's story

The image of the landau was very important to Bruno. Throughout his childhood he drew this picture again and again . . . *Notes to the company from Jacob Schulz, Bruno's nephew, June 1992*

Seduced by my mother's caresses, I forgot my father, and my life began to run along a new and different track with no holidays and no miracles. *The Book*

Maria   Dinner's ready.

Joseph *tries to pick* **Mother** *up.* **Maria** *pushes him away.*

Charles (*reprovingly*)   Joseph.

Maria *takes* **Mother** *on her back and moves slowly to the dinner table. The shop counter now becomes the table.* **Adela** *and* **Leon** *cover it with a tablecloth.* **Joseph** *remains DSR looking out at the audience in defeat.* **Mother** *sits.*

Joseph   Mother, I'm sorry Mother. I was trying to remember better times. (*He sits beside* **Mother**.) Times when we used to ride in our old landau.

Adela *and* **Maria** *USR of the table hand plates to* **Joseph** *who passes them to* **Mother**, **Agatha** *and* **Charles**. **Emil** *sits opposite SR of the table. Everyone is tired, dishevelled and forlorn.*

Mother   Ah, yes! We used to ride in our old landau with its enormous hood. At dusk we came to the thc last turning in the road. There was a rotting frontier post with a faded inscription on a board that was swaying in the wind. The wheels of the landau sank in the sand, the chattering spokes fell silent.

From SL, the **Assistants** *wheel in* **Father** *on a trolley. He is immobile, in a black coat, like a waxwork. During the speech, very slowly, they bring him to the table, without* **Joseph** *noticing.*

We paid the toll, the turnpike squeaked and we drove on into a forest. The trees were dry and smelled like cigars, the thickets were dry fluff and the leaves were tobacco-coloured. As we drove on the forest became darker and darker and smelled more and more aromatically of tobacco, until at last it enclosed us entirely like a box of havanas. The coachman couldn't light the lanterns. He had no matches. And breathing very heavily, the horses found their way home by instinct as we rolled on and on into . . . autumn.

5 Autumn

> Autumn is a huge touring show . . . it is a time of great confusion: everybody is pulling at the curtain ropes, and the sky, a great autumnal sky, hangs in tatters and is filled with the screeching of pulleys . . . there is an atmosphere of feverish haste, of belated carnival, a ballroom about to empty in the small hours, a panic of masked people who cannot find their real clothes. *A Second Fall*

Charles *takes off his hat out of which fall autumn leaves, lights a cigar and watches leaves fluttering down DSL.* **Maria** *and* **Adela** *part to reveal* **Father**.

Joseph (*turns to see his* **Father** *once more. He is delighted.*) Father . . . Father (*Turns to* **Mother**.) Mother, Father is still alive . . .

Mother   Of course he's still alive, he's at the dinner table.

Joseph   Father . . . How wonderful to see you. But why are you wearing your coat at the table, Father?

There is no response from **Father**. **Joseph** *sits down, despondent. Then he has an idea. He will try playing a joke he used to play with* **Father**.

Joseph   Father . . . do you remember?

He turns **Charles**'s *cigar round the wrong way.* **Charles**'s *response to sucking the hot coal is muted and automatic.*

Charles   Argh!

All look at **Joseph**.

Joseph (*goes to* **Father** *and clasps him by his hand*)   Father. Oh, Father. (*It is a dummy hand and comes away in his own. He throws it away in horror.*)

6   The Gale

Night came. The wind intensified in force and violence. There, in those charred, many-raftered forests of attics, darkness began to degenerate and ferment wildly . . . *The Gale*

The desks begin to shift, as if by themselves. **Joseph** *throws himself on to the desks, trying to gain control of the situation, as if his fantasy had a life of its own.*

Pots and pans begin to rattle in the attic.

All look up.

Charles   I think there's a storm brewing.

Emil   Un tornado!

Mother   You won't be going to school today, Joseph, there's a gale blowing.

Agatha   Close the shutters or we'll lose our soup!

Leon *goes to close the DSR doors, which are rattling.*

Charles   You know, Joseph, I remember a wind so strong we had to put brass pestles and flat irons in our pockets . . .

The door flies open as **Leon** *reaches it. A blast of wind blows the tablecloth and all the people into a great sideways-leaning picture.* **Father** *disappears SL. The door is slammed shut. Everyone is slumped over the table.* **Father** *has disappeared.*

Joseph   Father!

The hand that fell out of **Father**'*s arm rears up mysteriously and takes possession of the cloth, with* **Emil** *and* **Charles** *holding on to either side of it, it propels* **Joseph** *DSC where he seems to fight with this wooden hand. They move to the door to attempt to throw it away. The door bursts open once more. Another creature is caught in the sheet. A form pressing against it, like a furey. The sheet whips away, revealing a girl dressed in black. It is* **Maria** *with half a plate. The rest of the cast are blown by this blast to the USL corner.* **Joseph** *frantically tries to get to* **Maria**. *She is sucked once more out of the door. The rest of the cast are sucked back to their individual desks, which have come apart from the table. They slump over the desks. They are a grotesque repetition of the happy children in the first class. They look like Death. As* **Joseph** *goes to each desk in turn, it opens. Light pours out of it. They begin once more to repeat – mantra-like – 'Der Erlkönig'.*

Class
    'Wer reitet so spät durch Nacht und Wind?' . . .

Maria, *as the embodiment of the gale bursts in USL and threatens everyone as she comes DSL. The group staggers USR opposite* **Maria**. *The gale /* **Maria** *mocks* **Joseph** *and produces a half-broken plate.* **Joseph** *finds the other half in his pocket and approaches her with it in desperation. The group hold* **Joseph** *by his coat tails and flap as they cross diagonally to* **Maria**. **Maria** *removes her coat. She is naked beneath it. She is the ideal of the woman that* **Joseph** *dreams about and constantly draws.* **Joseph** *almost reaches her, their broken halves almost meet, but the gale capriciously whisks her half away at the last moment.* **Joseph** *falls. The group whirls away and disappears DSR.* **Joseph** *chases* **Maria** *through the* *desks and out DSR. As he shuts the door he still has a flapping shawl in his hands. He thrusts it into the stove. A jet of flame bursts from the stove.*

The sound of marching feet.

Joseph *returns to set desks in line facing the US wall. He is trying to reconstitute the shop as it was.*

Part Four: The Act of Destruction

1 The worshippers of Baal

> The time of the Great Season was approaching. The streets were getting busy. At six in the evening the city became feverish, the houses stood flushed, and people walked about made up in bright colours, illuminated by some interior fire, their eyes shining with a festive fever, beautiful yet evil. *The Night of the Great Season*

Joseph *alone behind the desks.*

The sound of marching feet dies away.

Joseph (*desperately tries the bell. It no longer rings.*)   Kling! Kling!

Doors fly open USL. Enter the shoppers. They are keen to buy. They walk describing an ominous square space around the shop.

Joseph   Hey! Hey! The shop is closed!

The shoppers continue to walk. **Joseph** *is confused. On the final side of the square, advancing from USC to DSL, the shoppers suddenly turn and point at* **Joseph***'s shop as if this is the one they want. They then peel round, one behind the other until they are in the USL corner, pointing at things in the shop, talking excitedly, imploring* **Joseph** *to open the shop and start selling to them. They come to the door. They knock on the windows looking at all the things that they want to buy.*

Theodore   Come on Joseph, open up, we've been here long enough.

Joseph   The shop is closed. Come back tomorrow!

Emil   Abri la tienda a hora!

Mother   Absolutely!

Joseph   I'm sorry but we are in the middle of stocktaking.

Leon   Auf die Tür! Heute schwimmen wir im Geld!

Everybody laughs.

Their chorus of demands to **Joseph** *to open the shop grow and grow until they break into song: 'Worthy is the Lamb' from Handel's* Messiah, *led by* **Charles**.

Charles   Joseph, Joseph, open the shop.

All (*laugh*)
Joseph, Joseph, open the shop.
For you must trade with us and sell us your cloth
To receive power and riches and wisdom and strength
And honour and glory and blessing.

(*Much quieter.*)
Joseph, Joseph, open the shop.

Joseph   Go away.

All
For you must trade with us and sell us your cloth
To receive power and riches and wisdom and strength
And honour and glory and blessing.

The group breaks once more into the cacophony of demands. **Leon** *finds the door handle, places it and orchestrates the group to all push together. They break into the shop. Slow motion.* **Theodore** *produces the bell and rings it. Bell and handle go into the stove. The group turns.*

All (*very delicate singing as they move forward to the position behind the desks*)
'Worthy is the Lamb that was slain
And hath redeemed us to God by his blood
To receive power and riches and wisdom and strength
And honour and glory and blessing.'

They advance towards the counter. They start to open the desks and look at what is inside. **Joseph** *tries to stop them and then gives up. In despair,* **Joseph** *takes his chair and sits.*
'Worthy is the Lamb that was slain
And hath redeemed us to God by his blood
To receive power and riches and wisdom and strength
And honour and glory and blessing.'

Theodore *and* **Leon** *slam DSR desktops shut. All straighten up.*

Mother   Well of course I saw them only very recently and you know what people say.

Agatha   A rolling stone gathers no moss.

Emil   Un artista! That's what he thinks he is.

Theodore   Which is exactly what I said last week.

A rhythmic cacophony of agreement and observation.

Charles (*sees what he is after*)   Well, look at that for a piece of cloth!

The shoppers burst through the counter. **Adela** *and* **Theodore** *throw themselves on to a big blue cloth DSL. They stretch it out in front of* **Joseph**, *who is surrounded by the other shoppers. They hold it up to him.* **Emil** *pulls a beautiful piece of cloth out of the flies SL whilst SR* **Charles** *unrolls the cloth that* **Father** *had put up in the first scene of the show. They cross each other, grabbing and tearing at them in their impatience.* **Father**, **Theodore**, **Charles**, **Emil**, **Leon** *raise* **Joseph**'s *chair and take him to the back wall where they place him on a chairlift, which winches him up overlooking the entire stage and the action, high up and powerless to intervene. Other white silks fall from the ceiling. They see high above USL a shelf containing cloth.*

Theodore   That's the one I want.

The shoppers build a tower of desks in order to try and reach this cloth USL. **Theodore** *climbs. His chair 'falls' to simulate a fake accident. It is caught by* **Charles** *or* **Emil** *who crashes to the ground in a mock fall.* **Theodore** *climbs on to pegs and then reaches the cloth. Shouted instructions between* **Mother**, **Joseph** *and* **Theodore**. *The landscape cloth tumbles. It covers the entire stage. The group stretch it out. It is supported by two poles, goes over the desks and is part attached to the original shelf where* **Theodore** *pulled it from and held in the lap of* **Joseph** *sitting halfway up the wall. It forms a huge landscape-like expanse on to which are projected moving cloud bursts.*

Joseph   'And when Moses saw this, his anger burned within him. And he threw the tables of the Commandments and he broke them at the foot of the Mountain. And he took the calf that they had made and burned it in the fire, ground it into powder and made the children of Israel drink it. And turning to Aaron he said, "What did these people unto thee, that thou hast brought so great a sin upon them?" And Aaron said "Let not the anger of my Lord wax hot. Thou knowest the people that they are set on mischief."'

From beneath the landscape, the group emerges holding books and ledgers above their heads like birds. They cross to DSR. **Joseph** *sees them and recognises some of the birds.*

2   The fall of birds

And soon the sky came out in a coloured rash, in blotches which grew and spread, and was filled with a strange tribe of birds. They were the distant, forgotten progeny of that generation of birds which at one time Adela had chased away to all four points of the sky. All of a sudden stones began to whistle through the air. The stupid, thoughtless people had begun to throw them into the fantastic bird-filled sky. *The Night of the Great Season*

Joseph   Father, the birds have come back, Father. Look! The condor and the wrens from England.

When they reach DSR the birds become people again. **Theodore** *appears as a bird at the top of ladder stage left.* **Emil** *throws a book directly at him.* **Theodore** *(as the bird) flaps and falls to the floor.* **Emil** *drags him centre stage in the middle of the white cloth. The black coats / the shoppers surround him and begin to stone him with books. He struggles and writhes on the sheet. The crowd fold up the cloth. It becomes very dark. The cloth is pulled very slowly in a procession DSR.* **Leon** *opens a trap door in the floor. Light pours out. There is no other light. Everybody and everything in the cloth gradually slides into the trap and disappears extremely slowly.* **Joseph** *has come off his seat on the back wall. He is clasping his chair to his chest. As the trap door closes, he sits on his chair DSC. He lifts his book. He is* *in the position that he was at the very beginning of the show. He looks out into the audience.*

Once more, the sound of marching feet.

Epilogue

19 November 1942

On a day I don't recall in 1942, known as Black Thursday in
Drohobycz, the Gestapo carried out a massacre in the ghetto. We
happened to be in the ghetto to buy food (instead of at work
outside). When we heard shooting and saw Jews run for their lives
we too took to flight. Schulz, physically the weaker, was caught by
a Gestapo agent called Guenther, who stopped him, put a
revolver to his head, and fired twice. *Letter to Jerzy Ficowski from
Tadeusz Lubowiecki, Gilwice, 1949.*

Upstage, across from one side to the other are nine chairs. **Joseph***'s
characters run from USL to USR and stop, each one standing beside a
chair. They are in this order:*

Adela Theodore Maria Leon Agatha Charles Emil Mother Father

The sound of marching feet fades away.

*The characters behind their chairs turn, look out into the audience and
sit down.* **Theodore** *begins to march whilst seated. The rest of the
characters join in with him. It is the same rhythm that we have heard
from marching feet all the way through the show.* **Joseph** *hears the
sound of marching feet and is frightened. He backs off upstage, running
to and fro as if he can now really see soldiers coming and closing in on
him; as if he is surrounded by a reality we cannot see. He finds himself
between the seated* **Leon** *and* **Agatha***.* **Leon** *holds him by the arm.*

Theodore Company halt!

The characters stop marching. **Agatha** *stands on her chair and makes
the sign of a gun against his temple. The sound of a real gunshot, loud.*
Joseph *staggers forward. His book drops beside him. He totters to
his chair. He takes off his jacket and drops it. Then his tie. He removes
his shoes. He returns to the end of the line upstage where he removes his
shirt and trousers. He falls into his* **Father***'s arms wearing only socks
and underpants. His* **Father** *cradles him like a baby and passes him
in this infant position to* **Mother***, next to him, where now we see that
he looks like a pieta. He is passed all the way along the line of actors.*

Adela, *the last, stands with him in her arms. She walks directly SL and the rest of the cast stand up. She turns downstage. The group gather round her. They gently walk a few steps towards the audience. They stop. With* **Joseph** *in her arms, for a moment, they look at the audience.* **Adela** *starts to walk backwards and gradually they all turn away and exit through the USL double doors.*

Disappearing into the light.

The Three Lives of Lucie Cabrol

The Three Lives of Lucie Cabrol was first performed at The Dancehouse Manchester on 12 January 1994, opening the Manchester City of Drama Festival. The play then toured to Theatre Royal Winchester, Oxford Playhouse, Gardner Arts Centre Brighton, Swan Theatre Stratford (RSC), Darlington Civic Theatre, Riverside Studios London and Theater Gessner Allee Zurich.

A 1995 revival toured to Shaftesbury Theatre London (West End season), Everyman Liverpool; Leicester Haymarket; Blackpool Grand Theatre;Theatre Royal, Bury St Edmunds; Newcastle Playhouse; Bouffes du Nord, Paris; Mercat de los Flores, Barcelona; Prinzregenten Theater, Munich; Schauspielhaus, Hamburg; Hebbel Theatre, Berlin; Kulturwerkstatt Kaserne, Basel; Helsinki Kansalllisteatteri; Bournemouth Festival at Poole Arts Centre; Stockholm Orionteater; Teatro Due, Parma; Tokyo Globe; Perth Octagon; Melbourne Festival; and was presented by the Sydney Theatre Company at the Seymour Centre, Sydney.

A 1996 revival toured to Lincoln Center Festival, New York; Teatro San Martin, Buenos Aires; Chicago Atheneum; Toronto Harbourfront Centre, Belgrade International Festival and the Macedonian National Theatre, Skopje.

Based on a story by John Berger
Adapted by Simon McBurney & Mark Wheatley
Devised by The Company

Director Simon McBurney
Design Tim Hatley
Lighting Paule Constable
Sound Christopher Shutt
Collaborators Annabel Arden and Annie Castledine

The original cast was as follows:

Lucie Cabrol, *the Cocadrille*	Lilo Baur
Jean	Simon McBurney
Marius Cabrol	Hannes Flaschberger
Mélanie Cabrol	Hélène Patarôt

Émile Cabrol/St Just	Stefan Metz
Henri Cabrol	Tim McMullan
Edmond Cabrol/André Masson	Mick Barnfather

The Company also played the land, animals, children, villagers and the dead. Some of the text was spoken in the actors' native languages where this was not English.

1995–6 Revival

Cast Lilo Baur, Mick Barnfather, Hannes Flaschberger, Michaela Granit, Paul Hamilton, Christine Marx, Simon McBurney, Tim McMullan, Stefan Metz, Hélène Patarôt

Awards

1994   TMA/Martini Award for Best UK Touring Production
1994   Time Out Theatre Award
1994   Manchester Evening News Award for Best Actress in a Visiting Production (Lilo Baur)
1995   Barcelona Critics Award for Best Foreign Production
1995   The Age Newspaper Critics Award for Creative Excellence at the Melbourne International Festival
1996   Belgrade Daily Newspaper Politika Prize for Best Director
1996   Best Performance of the Belgrade International Festival, voted by the audience
1996   Grand Prix of the Belgrade International Festival
1997   Toronto DORA Award for Best Actress (Lilo Baur)
1997   Toronto DORA Award for Best Production of a Play

Thanks to all those who have contributed to the production over the years: Paul Anderson, Anita Ashwick, Ian Beswick, Sophie Brech, Johanna Coe, Judith Dimant, Henrietta Duckworth, Judith Edgeley, Sandra Formica, Sue Gibbs, Nicole Griffiths, Sarah-Jane Hughes, Rodger Hulley, John

Mackinnon, Jane Martin, Catherine Reiser, Ian Richards, Alison Ritchie, Russell Warren-Fisher.

Part One

Prologue

Music. The stage is covered in earth. All sit upstage except **Jean**. *In front of them pairs of boots irregularly placed. Running water, stage left.* **Jean** *enters. He washes, drinks a little, and comes down centre.*

Jean (*indicating a pair of boots*) Émile Cabrol, who died of his war wounds nearly twenty years after the Great War. Émile. Eldest son of (*indicating another pair of boots*) Marius Cabrol and his wife la Mélanie. (*Another pair.*) Henri Cabrol, second son of Marius and La Mélanie, who was to say of his sister, 'This woman has never brought anything but shame on my family.' (*Another pair.*) My schoolteacher, André Masson, who died in the mud at Verdun. (*He gestures towards other pairs.*) Joset, swept away by an avalanche. St Just, the betrayed marquisard who was shot, and Georges, who electrocuted himself because he knew he would become a pauper. The dead surround the living, and the living form the core of the dead.

Villager 1 (*sings through a makeshift loud-hailer*)
 Like a trout
 our mountain basks
 in the setting sun

 as the light drains
 the trout dies
 its mouth open

 the night
 with its wings of spruce
 flies the mountain
 to the dead
 to the dead
 Ave Maria
 Ave Maria

All come forward and put on their boots. They lift a tin bath and circle in a funeral procession. **Jean** *sits at his stove.*

Jean   Before I was six, perhaps I was only two or three, I would collect the sticks for my father on winter mornings when it was still as dark as night. We kneeled by this iron beast, feeding it. Now when I light the stove in the morning, I say to myself: I and the fire are the only living things in this house; my father, mother, brothers, sisters, the horse, cows, rabbits, chickens, all have gone. And Lucie Cabrol, who was known as the Cocadrille, is dead.

With a crash like thunder, **Lucie** *is rolled out of her coffin and squats silent.*

1   Birth

Jean   The Cocadrille was born in 1900. It's the month of September 1900 . . .

All take off their outer clothes to reveal the cloths of 1900. **Marius** *harnesses up his horse and begins ploughing.*

The Cabrol farm is on a slope above our village which is called Brine.

Marius *ploughs and then begins turning over the earth by hand.*

Marius   That day white cloud, like smoke, was blowing through the open door of the stable. Marius Cabrol was milking.

La Mélanie *and* **Émile** *are revealed in turn.*

La Mélanie   His wife . . .

Marius (*pointing her out*)   La Mélanie.

La Mélanie   . . . was in bed, on the other side of the stable wall, attended by her brother and a neighbour.

Émile   Their first child had been a boy, christened Émile.

Marius   Marius hoped that his second child would also be a boy and he would name him Henri after his grandfather.

La Mélanie   The baby was born very quickly.

Jean *scatters a bucket of potatoes. All gather as if at the stable door.*

Marius   It's a girl.

La Mélanie   Give her to me. Jesus, forgive me! She's marked with the mark of the craving.

Villager 1   She is. It's red. It's burning.

La Mélanie   She is. It's a mark. I've been punished. I've marked her.

Marius   Calm down, La Mélanie. It's where her face rubbed when she came out.

Villager 2   I've never seen a mark like that before.

La Mélanie   I've been punished.

Marius   Stop it, woman. It's nothing. It'll be gone in a few weeks.

Pause.

Villager 3   She's minute.

Villager 1   She's a dwarf.

Villager 3   She's like a dwarf but she's not.

Villager 1   If she's like a dwarf, she must be a dwarf.

Marius   No, she's just tiny.

La Mélanie   She's like a little red radish.

Marius *takes the mark from* **Lucie**'s *face.*

Marius   In a few days the red mark did disappear.

La Mélanie   But La Mélanie thought she had been marked in another way.

Lucie *runs off.*

La Mélanie   You lose her as easily as you lost a button.

Villager 3 *sings a work song. All begin picking potatoes.* **Lucie** runs in grabbing a pig.

Lucie   Soyley, soyley! Papa! The pig, the pig, the pig!

All seize the pig and take it squealing to the bathtub where it is slaughtered. **Villager 3** *cuts its throat. The men butcher it, keeping* **Lucie** *away.*

Marius   Lucie, Lucie. (*He gives her the pig's tail.*)

The women take buckets of offal to the other side of the stage where they pour it all into one to clean it and make blood sausage.

La Mélanie (*to* **Lucie**)   You see, nothing's wasted in a pig. Pick that up, there . . . To make the best black pudding you have to clean it properly, get rid of all the muck, see? (*She demonstrates cleaning the intestine.*) Look at that, it's a lot bigger than last year . . .

Lucie *pulls at a piece of the intestine, playing with it like rubber.*

La Mélanie   Leave it alone! Go and empty the buckets!

The men go to the back where they stretch the pig's skin, a leather jacket, over two sticks. **Lucie** *plays and talks to the pig's tail. The school bell sounds, softly at first (sound made by striking the milk churn).*

Lucie (*to the dead pig*)   What are you doing? What are you doing in there? You're quiet now. You're quiet now because soon you're going to be bacon!

Pig sits up in the bath, dripping wet. He gets out and becomes **Henri**.

Henri   Soon after Lucie was born, La Mélanie did have another child – and this time it was a boy and he *was* christened Henri, after his grandfather.

He puts his shirt and braces on.

By the time he was three he was already bigger than his sister. (*To* **Lucie**.) Give me that pig's tail. Go on, give it to me.

He takes the bucket **Lucie** *is carrying and throws it to another of the children. They tease her.*

Children   Lucie, Lucie . . . ! Here, Lucie . . . !

She can't get it back. They go into the classroom and sit on their buckets for chairs. She follows, last, having retrieved her bucket from the corner where it was thrown.

2   The name of the Cocadrille

Masson *teaches his class.*

Masson   Bonjour, class.

Children   Bonjour, Monsieur Masson.

Masson *writes on the board.*

Children   Wednesday September the tenth, nineteen ten . . . o-ten . . .

Jean   Ten!

Masson   Now, the catechism. What is avarice? Joset, let's give someone else a chance. Jean. Avarice, please!

Jean   Me, Monsieur Masson? Oh . . . Avarice is – Avarice is –

Joset   A big mountain.

Masson   Avarice is. Good, let's start there, shall we!

Jean   We'll start there, shall we. Avarice is –

Lucie   Avarice is an excessive longing for the good things of life especially money.

Masson   Good, Lucie. And is the love of the good things of life ever justified?

Lucie   Always. When it inspires thrift and foresight.

Masson   Good. *Only* when it inspires thrift and foresight.
Now, were we all listening?

Children   Avarice is an excessive longing for the good
things of life especially money . . . especially money . . .
especially money . . .

They repeat it more and more softly until only **Lucie***'s voice is heard,
as we go into a work scene with the family and villagers.*

Lucie   Love of the good things of life is justified only when
it inspires thirst and foresight.

Henri *holds his bucket above* **Lucie***'s head.*

Henri   Henri hated his sister.

He brings it crashing down as **Lucie** *runs to work with her father.*
Marius *chops wood on a block down left.* **Lucie** *chops beside him.
Two other villagers bring up the wood.* **Marius** *sees* **Henri** *not
working.*

Marius   Henri. Work.

Henri *crouches beside his sister and picks up the wood she has
chopped.*

Henri   Do all these bits again. They should be like this,
see? (*Picking up a potato.*) I'm going to do this potato. Then
I'm going to do your leg. (*He chops the potato.*)

La Mélanie *goes off and returns after a moment, calling to*
Marius.

La Mélanie   Marius! Marius! Three of my chickens are
dead.

Marius   What was it – a weasel?

La Mélanie   No. There's not a mark on them.

Marius   A fox?

La Mélanie   No, it wasn't a fox.

Marius   What was it then?

Henri   Lucie killed them.

Lucie   I didn't touch them.

Henri   She did. She looked at them and they died.

All laugh and go back to work.

She did, she did. She looked at them and they died. She's a
cocadrille. That's what a cocadrille is. She can kill things by
looking at them. She was born in a dung heap and she
smells. She's a cocadrille.

Lucie   I'm not.

Henri   She's a cocadrille. She's a cocadrille.

Lucie   I'm not.

Henri *threatens her with a stick.*

Henri   Let's play Cocadrilles. Say you're a cocadrille.

He beats his stick around her. Then he hits the bucket she is carrying.

Say it. Say it! You're a cocadrille. Say it!

Lucie *leaps at him. They fight.* **Marius** *and* **La Mélanie** *shouts
at their children and then have to separate them.* **La Mélanie** *gives*
Lucie *a postcard.*

La Mélanie   Lucie, read this for me. Go on . . .

Lucie (*reading*)   'I am coming home. Émile.' Émile is
coming home.

La Mélanie   When?

Lucie   Friday.

La Mélanie   Friday.

School bell begins to sound.

Lucie   Émile. Émile is coming home from Paris.

Jean *looks over her shoulder.*

Jean   Émile Cabrol.

All form class again on their buckets.

Masson   Bonjour, class.

Children   Bonjour, Monsieur Masson.

Masson   Lucie, take your place. Thank you.

Lucie *sits.* **Masson** *writes on the board.*

Children   Friday September the fourteenth, nineteen twelve.

Henri *spits at* **Lucie** *and taunts her.*

Masson   Something to say, Henri?

Henri   Lucie was born in a dung heap. That's why she stinks of shit. She's a cocadrille. She can kill anything she looks at. She comes from a cock's egg. That's what a cocadrille is. She killed a badger on the road the other day.

Masson *begins writing on the board.*

Masson   Insults!

Children read what he has written.

Children   Insults should be written on sand.

Masson   Compliments, Henri . . .

Children   Compliments should be inscribed on marble.

Lucie *runs outs.* **Masson** *calls after her.*

Masson   Lucie. Lucie! Lucie!

His calls cross-fade with **Émile**'s *in the distance.*

Émile   Lucie! Lucie!

Lucie *stands centre.* **Émile** *changes his costume in the class. He climbs. He teases her by stopping. She yells at him.*

Lucie   Émile! É-mile! Did you see it?

Émile   What?

Lucie   The Eiffel Tower.

Émile   You see it everywhere. It's more than three hundred metres high.

They continue calling, getting nearer until **Lucie** *jumps into his arms. The class has dissolved.* **Marius** *and* **La Mélanie** *greet* **Émile**. **Henri** *sits.*

Marius (*not knowing what to say*)   Good. Paris. Snow came early this year.

La Mélanie   Oh, enough! Leave him alone. (*To* **Émile**.) Take your coat off. Sit down. Eat. What did you eat in Paris? Not much, eh?

She brings **Émile** *to the table. He plays with* **Lucie** *and* **Henri**. *He eats in silence. They watch.*

Émile   This bread. Shepherd's bread. You never get bread like this in Paris. (*To* **Henri**.) Do you know how many horses there are in Paris?

Lucie   Three hundred and seventy-one.

Émile   Two million.

Marius *cuffs him on the head.*

Marius (*derisively*)   Two million. Two million! (*Laughing.*) That's a lot of shit!

Goes back to his work.

Émile (*to the others*)   In Paris there is a metro too. The metro is a train that goes underground. Parisians are lazy – they can't get out of bed in the mornings. You should see them running along the tunnels to catch their trains. (*Looking at* **Henri**, *he puts a silver-painted model of the Eiffel Tower in front of* **Lucie**.) On a clear night you can see more lights in the city than there are stars in the sky.

Lucie   Did you climb to the top?

Émile   What top?

Lucie   The top of the Eiffel Tower!

Émile   You go up by lift.

Lucie   Lift?

Émile   Yes, a lift.

Lucie   What's lift?

The others laugh.

What's lift?

Henri   The Cocadrille knows nothing! The proper place for her is her dung heap.

Lucie *gets up, finds a pail of milk, picks it up and hurls the milk into* **Henri**'s *face.*

Lucie   If you weren't a weasel, I'd kill you!

La Mélanie   Marius!

Marius *comes in from milking. He catches* **Lucie** *by the ear and takes her round the table to the corner. He beats her.*

Marius   Milk is not water! Milk is not water!

La Mélanie   Marius!

He stops. He strides back to his work. **Lucie** *comes over to him and watches. After a moment* **Marius** *can't ignore her. He picks her up and holds her.*

Marius   Ah, my Cocadrille! My Cocadrille. (*To* **La Mélanie**.) I know – she just came out like that, didn't she? I know she can't help it.

He pinches **Lucie**'s *cheek.*

She just came out like that. My Cocadrille. My Cocadrille! My Cocadrille! My Cocadrille!

He dances with her, spinning round and round. Then he puts her down and she runs with the other children.

Jean   And so the name Cocadrille, born of both hatred and love, replaced the name Lucie.

Children   The Cocadrille! The Cocadrille!

The children's chanting turns nasty as the school bell begins to sound.

Cocadrille! Cocadrille! Cocadrille!

They line up to form the class, which **Masson** *walks through.*

Masson   Bonjour, class.

The others sit on their buckets. **Jean** *takes* **Masson**'s *coat as he writes on the board.*

Jean   August the eleventh 1914.

Masson   André Masson was killed at Verdun. Each morning he wrote on the board the day of the week, the date of the month and the year of the century. On the war memorial there is only the month and the year of his death. March 1916.

The class begin scything where they sit and slowly get up.

3   The First War and the birth of Edmond

The family is scything on the slopes. The stick held by one strikes the spade held by another. A tolling bell.

Marius   The war has started.

The family look down left as if tracing the source of the sound in the valley below.

La Mélanie   The massacre of the world has begun.

Marius *goes to* **La Mélanie**. *He gives her his stick which is taken by* **Lucie**.

Marius   I'll be back before the snow. I'll be back.

He marches upstage. **Jean** *runs downstage, excited.*

Jean   Émile, Émile, I got my mobilisation papers.

Émile   Where did you get them?

Jean   They're in the village.

The others follow him, **Émile** *last. Cheers. They begin singing as they march off to war.* **Marius** *joins the end of their procession reluctantly.*

Men
  Oh-U, oh-U, oh-Ursula
  Pour toi d'amour mon c[oe]ur brule
  Il faudrait l'énergie d'une pompe à vapeur
  Pour éteindre le feu qui consume mon c[oe]ur

They continue until they stand upstage. They suddenly stop singing in mid-march. Freeze.

La Mélanie   Marius did not come back before the snow came, nor before the new year, nor before the spring. The endless time of war began.

Lucie   Maman!

La Mélanie   La Mélanie, the Cocadrille and Henri were left to run the farm.

Lucie *works.* **Henri** *stands on the table watching. The men resume their song faintly and march on the spot.*

La Mélanie   The Cocadrille was tireless. She was not the second woman of the house, she was more like a hired hand – a man.

Lucie *drives the horse.*

Henri   A midget man with a difficult and unpredictable character.

La Mélanie   She drove the mare, she fetched the wood, she milked the cows, she dug the garden. She mended the harnesses. She could carry eighty kilos of hay on top of her head. But she never washed clothes nor sewed.

Henri   There was so much to be done that for three years Henri could no longer afford to quarrel openly with his sister.

Lucie *continues working. Song rises.* **Émile** *screams.*

Lucie   Émile. Émile.

Lucie *rushes to buckets for milking.*

I will milk nine, no ten, buckets a day, to keep you alive. (*To the milk.*) Keep him alive. Keep Émile alive. Émile, come back. Come back. (*She prays.*) Our Father, Who art in heaven, Hallowed be Thy name . . .

Émile *is carried home.* **Lucie** *looks at him and follows him. She pushes* **Henri** *off his chair and* **Émile** *is seated. She gives him soup.*

Jean   No one in the village spoke of victory. They only spoke of the war being ended.

Le Mélanie *waits for* **Marius**.

La Mélanie   Marius. Marius!

Unseen, he watches her and walks towards her. He grabs her from behind and lifts her into the air. **Lucie** *goes to get* **Marius**'s *stick.*

Émile   A baby, at her age!

Marius   It will be her last.

Lucie   Papa.

Lucie *gives* **Marius** *his stick and another. He harnesses* **La Mélanie**.

Emile   It will have to be!

Marius   All the war I promised myself that.

He begins ploughing.

Émile   So we'll be four. The farm will be divided into four.

Henri   Only if you count the Cocadrille.

Émile   Oh, shut up! (*To* **Marius**.) Have you told the Cocadrille?

Marius   Not yet. It's for Mother to tell her.

Émile   It'll change the Cocadrille. Me and the Cocadrille, we might be married now with our own children.

Edmond *lands on* **Marius**'s *back as he ploughs.*

Émile   Yet who is going to marry the Cocadrille? And I'm too sick to marry. It ought to be our turn and, instead, you've made another baby.

Marius (*smiling*)   Call it an old man's last sin!

Marius *turns and goes upstage.* **Edmond** *drops centre and stands beside* **Henri**.

Edmond   In September 1919 La Mélanie had her fourth child, a boy, who was christened . . .

Henri *gives him a lit cigarette. He takes a puff* . . . Edmond.

4   The mountain pastures

Jean *comes from upstage.*

Jean   Now, every summer the village took all the cattle up to the mountain pastures, the alpage.

The sound of the cows and goats.

Up there it was mostly the young women who looked after the cows and goats.

The young men get ready to climb the mountain. They strap upturned chairs to their backs for haversacks, provisions.

It was the unmarried daughter who had the pair of hands most easily spared from the work in the valley below. And from time to time a visiting priest would preach a sermon against the immorality of leaving young women alone in the alpage.

The men put on their hats.

Man 1   Joset.

Man 2   Véronique.

Man 3   Rosemarie

Man 4   La belle Jacqueline.

Jean   La Nan Bessons.

La Mélanie *stands on the table, centre.*

La Mélanie   Old women still talk of their summers in the alpage.

She comes down helped by **Men** *as they begin their 'climb' up towards the table.*

Their summers in the alpage.

Men *climb on to and over the table and back until they stand on top.*

Man 4   You can see André's sheep from here.

Man 1   He's slow is André.

Man 3   He's slowed down since the death of Honorine.

Jean   He should marry again, and you know who to –

All   Who?

Jean   The maid of the priest, the enormous –

All   Philomène!

They laugh. They make the sound of the birds flapping and watch them fly past. **La Mélanie***, watching down right, picks up the bird sounds and sends them back again.* **Men** *repeat the names of their women. They set out to climb again.*

Man 4   No, no, not that way. The Cocadrille has her chalet up there. We'll have to go round.

They climb and stop at a water trough down left. As they turn to go,
Lucie *appears in front of them.* **Man 2** *is playing with his harmonica.*

Lucie   You have a harmonica.

Man 2   Yes, we have.

Lucie   I can dance.

Jean   Not in those sabots, you can't!

She kicks them off and dances, singing.

Lucie
  Apricagot de lee nay-a
  Sopiya-a, *etc.*

(*A mountain peasant song in a dead language.*)

The **Men** *join in.*

Jean   Stop! The music will tell the other girls that we are
here, then the surprise is ruined.

They stop.

We must go.

Lucie   Can one of you help me to move a barrel?

All   Go on, Georges . . .

Lucie   No, not you, I want the one who has just come
back from the army.

Men *laugh.*

All   Go on, Jean . . . La Nan Bessons! . . .

Jean (*to the others*)   You tell La Nan I'm definitely coming to
visit her! Definitely!

All   Definitely!

Jean *reluctantly goes to* **Lucie**. *The others laugh and go.*

Lucie   Let them go.

Lucie's *chalet is made with planks upright to one side and the table on the other. Behind the planks we hear the cows and goats crying and stamping in their stable.*

Jean (*awkwardly*)   You know what they say about you in the village? They say, she's so small she could get a job as a chimney sweep.

Lucie   I'm a woman and I'd shit down their chimneys.

Jean   Right!

Jean *begins to move the barrel, putting all his weight behind it. He discovers it is light and moves it easily.*

Lucie   Are you going away to Paris this autumn?

Jean   Yes.

She gives him a small glass and pours him some gnole. She drinks from the bottle.

Lucie   Will you go up the Eiffel Tower?

Jean   Maybe. I must be going. The others will be waiting.

Lucie   They're singing, can't you hear?

Distant harmonica.

I'll fetch you some butter.

Jean   We don't need any.

Lucie   You have so much at home that you can refuse butter?

She leaves and goes through into the stable, returning moments later. She no longer has any clothes on the upper half of her body. Her breasts are covered with milk. **Jean** *begins to run, returns for his hat, and stops. He kneels and licks the milk from her. Then he stands and runs out of the chalet and down the mountainside. His flight is made by a succession of chairs and the milk churn placed in his way. He runs over them and through them. He sits, panting.*

Jean   What was it that made me go back the following
night? Why did I deliberately go up alone, avoiding my
companions?

He 'climbs' back up and goes into the chalet. The sound of the animals.

Lucie   So you've finished the butter!

Jean   Can I have some more?

Lucie   Yes, Jean.

*She gives **Jean** some milk and spills it down his chest. A crash of
thunder. He takes off his shirt. She wipes her hand on him and licks
him. They play. He lifts her. They crash into the wall of planks. And
then through them. They roll back on under the planks. The planks
swing above them and drop in front of them. The planks slow to a
gentle swinging motion until they make a door which, after a moment,
Jean opens. **Jean** and **Lucie** go through it and sit.*

Jean   We played and made love on the wooden stage of
the bed as though we possessed the strength of the whole
village.

A stream flows down one of the planks.

Lucie   So, my goat, with me you can climb.

Jean *plays the goat.*

Lucie   The stars, Jean, look. They're so close, I could pick
you one.

*They go to the stream and drink and throw water at each other. They
lie down.*

When my brothers divide the farm, I'll get the slopes, the
part they don't want. The steep part. Nobody'll marry me,
Jean. Too steep. But you, my goat, you can climb!

Jean *lifts his head suddenly as if not sure what he's heard. Then he
gets up and begins getting ready to go.*

Lucie   Jean?

Jean   Lucie, I'm not going to come up again.

Lucie I didn't expect you to, Jean.

Jean It wasn't true that she would never marry. She was plotting to make me her husband. She believed she was already pregnant and I would be forced to marry her. Asleep in my bed I dreamed of her.

He runs down the mountainside. This time around the space. Until he falls on to the table and draws a blanket over him and sleeps. After a moment, **Lucie** *rushes in and perches on the edge of the table bed. All join her and stand around him. His dream:*

Lucie Only one man can be the father of my child and that is you, Jean!

Father Is it true? With the Cocadrille? I don't believe it.

Lucie I can prove it.

Father Then prove it!

Lucie I counted the moles on the small of his back.

Father How many are there?

Lucie Seven.

Father Seven! Then we will count them.

They pull down **Jean**'s *trousers, bend him over the table, and count.*

One, two, three, four, five, six . . . there are only six.

Jean There's only six.

Father Seven! You've ruined your life! Ruined it for nothing!

They withdraw. **Marius** *appears with a pail of milk. He falls. The milk spills.* **Jean** *wakes and screams.* **Lucie** *screams and runs to* **Marius**. **La Mélanie** *and the others join her and mourn* **Marius**.

Lucie Papa! Papa!

She prays over him. They life him in a funeral procession.

5   Marius's funeral and Marie

Jean (*getting up and folding his blanket*) - I woke up frightened and sweating. And when I saw her again, six months later, it was at her father's funeral. I looked closely and, to my relief, she was not pregnant. But by then, I had already made up my mind. I was going to leave the village. That was in the summer of 1924.

Lucie *comes to* **Jean** *from the procession.*

Lucie   So you are leaving us?

Jean   You were right, I am going to Paris. I might even go up the Eiffel Tower – who knows. Then maybe to South America.

Lucie   Come back before you die.

She rejoins the procession which goes upstage.

Émile   The years passed. In 1936 Émile died as the final consequences of his war wounds.

Émile *takes off his jacket and goes to the back of the procession.*

La Mélanie   Two years later La Mélanie followed her husband and her eldest son into the grave.

She puts her apron around **Lucie** *and goes to the back of the procession where she removes her top clothes to become* **Marie**. **Lucie** *stands and sharpens her scythe.*

Henri   The farm was divided up. It was shared between Edmond, Henri and the Cocadrille.

Henri *stands opposite* **Lucie** *sharpening his scythe.*

Lucie (*to scythe*)   For twenty summers I've cherished you like a son. If they gave me money, I could never find another one like you.

Henri   Henri married Marie.

Edmond   A woman from the next village.

Cheers. Rice is thrown over **Marie** *as she is lifted on to the table with a bundle containing lunch. She comes down and hands it to* **Henri** *and* **Edmond**.

Marie   Hey, here it is, lunch! And don't tell me I'm late because it's me who's done all the work again this morning. I fed the chickens, scrubbed the floor, stacked the wood. You should tell her I'm not madam's skivvy.

They sit without **Lucie**. **Lucie** *goes to join them and picks up the water and drinks.*

Marie   Better bring the hay in fast. It's going to rain, it's hot.

Lucie   However much you drink when you're making hay, you never piss!

She goes back to work.

Marie   She's as dirty as a chicken house. And she never lifts a finger in the kitchen. What kind of woman is that?

Henri *and* **Edmond** *go back to work. They scythe. They freeze together.*

Henri   The years passed. The Second War broke out.

6   The maquisards

Henri, **Edmond** *and* **Lucie** *scything.* **Henri** *looks up and sees two men watching them.*

Peasant from the Dranse   Good morning.

Henri   Shit!

Edmond   They're maquisards.

Henri   What else could they be?

Edmond   Jesus! We can't let anyone else see them.

Peasant from the Dranse   Two of us need shelter for
twenty-four hours.

Turns to **Lucie**.

Good morning, little girl.

She turns.

I'm sorry, madame, I didn't see –

Lucie   This is also my farm.

Lucie *continues to work.*

Edmond   Where are you from?

Peasant from the Dranse   From the Dranse. The SS
burned down my father's farm there.

Henri   All right, you can have some food but after that
you must go.

Peasant from the Dranse   No, we need to stay till
tomorrow. The comrade here has a wound that needs
dressing.

Edmond   Too bad.

Henri   We are not a hospital.

Lucie   I can dress it for you.

Henri   And if the Germans come?

Marie   He can't be in the house.

Peasant from the Dranse   No, he's right. Better we
stay up here. (*To* **Lucie**.) Can you, madame, get some hot
water and bandages. Please go, quickly.

The sound of an armoured car approaching.

Edmond   The Germans! What are we going to do?

Lucie   Take this. (*Hands him a stick.*) Work!

Henri   Work. Work! (*To the second maquisard*, **St Just**.)
Take that scythe and don't look up.

The car sound gets louder. The maquisards pretend to work.

The car is now very close. It passes. **St Just** *falls.*

Henri   Get up. Work!

Peasant from the Dranse   Leave him!

Lucie   It's safe now. They won't come back. (*To* **St Just**.)
You can go and rest in the hayloft.

Henri   And if they come back and find him?

Lucie   If they come back he can pretend to be working.

Henri   And if he's asleep?

Lucie   I'll stay with him.

Henri   Stay with him! You'll stay here and get his hay in.

Lucie *wheels the wheelbarrow downstage.* **Henri** *stops her, banging the stick of his scythe into the front of the barrow.*

It's not your farm they'll burn down. It's mine!

A stand-off. Moments pass. **Lucie** *looks at him.* **Henri** *moves away.* **Lucie** *helps* **St Just** *into the barrow and wheels him round and back downstage.* **The Peasant from the Dranse** *goes with them and keeps guard. Lighting changes to barn.* **Lucie** *undresses* **St Just** *and begins bathing his wound.*

Lucie   What is your first name?

St Just   They call me St Just.

Lucie   I have never heard that name. Rest now, St Just.

St Just   You have very gentle hands.

Lucie   Gentle! They've been in too much shit to be gentle.
How old are you?

St Just   Nineteen.

Peasant from the Dranse   The wound near the top of his thigh was like a wound of any generation. It was as red as raw beef.

Lucie   Is your mother still alive?

St Just   I believe so.

Lucie   Is your father still alive?

St Just   He is a judge.

Lucie   What will you do when the war stops?

St Just   I will continue my studies.

Lucie   And one day become a judge like your father?

St Just   No, it is another kind of justice that I believe in, a popular justice, a justice for peasants like you and for workers . . .

Lucie *squeezes a bloody sponge on to his bare thigh.*

. . . A justice which gives factories to those who work in them, and the land to those who cultivate it.

Lucie   Is your father rich?

St Just   Fairly.

Lucie   Won't you inherit some of his money one day?

St Just   All of it when he dies.

Lucie   There's the difference between us.

St Just   I shall use the money to start a paper. By then we shall have a free press. A free press is a prerequisite for the full mobilisation of the masses.

Lucie (*taking off her shoes*)   Really? Are *your* feet hot too?

St Just (*laughing*)   The hay is dusty.

Lucie   Meanwhile you are in danger.

St Just   Not more than you.

Lucie   That is true. Today we are equal.

St Just   Your brothers – do they think like you?

Lucie   I don't think.

St Just   I didn't trust them.

Lucie   They are as straight as a goat's hind leg. You must rest now . . . St Just.

She gives him something to drink.

St Just   I feel much stronger. Sit beside me, please sit down.

She sits with him. He lays his head in her lap. She strokes his hair.

You have very gentle hands.

Lucie   It's like raking hay!

The Peasant from the Dranse *lifts* **St Just** *and they stand together.*

Peasant from the Dranse   The two maquisards left the next day. Within forty-eight hours the village heard that a group of maquisards had been surprised in their camp, taken prisoner and shot.

Henri *comes forward to chop wood.*

Henri   Within forty-eight hours the village heard that a group of maquisards had been surprised in their camp by the milice, taken into the fields and shot. It was said that they would never have been found unless they had been tipped off by an informer.

He chops wood. Blood is thrown on **St Just**. **Lucie** *screams. She throws the wheelbarrow over. She puts* **St Just**'s *cartridge belt over her head and runs, carrying the rest of his clothes.*

7   The casting out

Henri, **Edmond** *and* **Marie** *sit and eat.* **Lucie** *enters, sobbing.*

Marie   She's as dirty as a chicken house. And she never lifts a finger in the kitchen. What kind of woman is that? In God's name, stop it woman! A woman of your age should be ashamed!

Edmond   Those who sleep with dogs, wake up with fleas!

Henri (*lighting a cigarette*)   That's good! Those who sleep with dogs, wake up with fleas!

Lucie *goes. She chops wood, brings it back and bangs a piece on to each of their plates. She empties a bucket of potatoes on to the table. She mimics ploughing with the harness sticks and throws them on to the table. She picks up a bucket of milk.*

Lucie   No. No!

And pours it away. She throws the milk churn off. All the while she curses them and sobs. She crouches down left. **Henri** *begins sniffing suspiciously and then discovers the red of a fire beneath them.*

Henri   Fire. Fire in the barn!

The noise of a large fire. Its red glow. **Edmond** *and* **Marie** *leap up from the table. All beat out the fire.* **Henri** *comes forward.*

Henri   This woman, this sister, has never brought anything but shame on my family.

Lucie *prays.*

Lucie   Maman. Papa. You should have known your sons better.

Henri   She started by stealing from us. Now she steals from our neighbours.

Lucie   You always thought of them as they were when they were in the cradle.

Henri   She never does any work any more.

Lucie   Shit! You didn't known where their evil came from.

Henri   If she lived in a city, she'd have been put in an institution years ago!

Lucie   You died, Papa, not knowing that to make a child you need a woman, a man and the devil!

Henri, **Marie** *and* **Edmond** *are seated at the table.*

Henri   The mayor was reluctant to refer the arson of the Cabrol barn to any outside authority.

Marie   It was the mayor's wife who came up with the solution which he finally proposed to Henri and Edmond. They accepted it enthusiastically.

Edmond *comes round the table, sweeps the debris from it and sits in* **Lucie***'s place.*

Marie   And with this proposal the first life of the Cocadrille came to an end.

Lucie *walks. She is loaded up with possessions – a sack, a spade, a chair, a blanket, her scythe – until she is bent under their weight. She circles the space and goes off up right. Fade.*

Part Two

8 Jean's return (forty years later)

Sound of the wind. All sit upstage. **Lucie** *enters with a sack. She takes out a Marlboro and smokes.* **Jean** *enters with a haversack. He watches her through binoculars.* **Lucie** *begins picking. The others come forward and make the bushes.*

Jean In the hot airless nights in Buenos Aires, when I lived on the fourteenth floor, not far from one of the worst shanty towns in the city, I used to stand at my window and dream of an Alpine summer. After twenty-five years in the Argentine, I went north to Montreal where I had a bar and for a while, I was rich. Sometimes I used to tell my story about Lucie Cabrol and her chalet in the alpage and those years in the moonlight. A client said to me, 'So this woman you were with, was she a dwarf?' 'No,' I said, 'She was like a dwarf, she was underdeveloped, she was ignorant, but she wasn't exactly a dwarf.' 'Well,' he said, 'if she was like a dwarf, she must have been a dwarf.' 'No,' I replied, 'she was just tiny.' But since my return to the village I had only heard of the Cocadrille from others.

Lucie *squats to shit and sees him.*

Lucie The passer-by should always raise his hat to the one who is shitting!

Jean *takes off his beret. She laughs and comes towards him.*

It's Jean! Do you recognise me?

Jean You're the Cocadrille.

Lucie No! Why are you following me?

Jean I came up here to look for mushrooms, for bolets.

Lucie You found some?

Jean What?

Lucie   Did you find some?

Jean   Yes.

Lucie   Give them to me.

Jean   What for?

Lucie   They are mine!

He closes his sack. She turns away, muttering.

So you've come back.

Jean   Yes, I've come back.

Lucie (*staring at him*)   You were away too long.

Jean   I remembered the way up here.

Lucie   You came up here to spy on me.

Jean   Spy?

Lucie   Spy on me!

Jean   Why should I want to spy on you?

Lucie   Give me the bolets then.

Jean   No. They're mine.

She curses him and continues picking raspberries.

Lucie   Whilst you were away, everything changed.

Jean   I suppose a lot must have changed when you left the farm.

Lucie   I didn't leave it. They threw me out.

Jean   I know.

Lucie   Did you marry out there?

Jean   Yes, I did.

Lucie   Why did you come back alone then?

Jean   Because my wife died.

Lucie (*crosses herself*)   Oh. You're a widower.

Jean   I am a widower.

Lucie   Do you have children?

Jean   Two boys. They are both working in the United States.

Lucie   America. America. Money can change everything. Money can eat and dance. Money can make the dirty clean. Money can make the dwarf big. I have two million!

Jean   I hope you keep it in a bank!

Lucie   Fuck off! Fuck off and get away!

She strides off, taking his haversack with her. The bushes now become a flock of birds disturbed by her. They squawk and fly off.

Jean   Wait! I need my haversack!

Lucie   You know where I live!

Jean   And when I looked again, she had vanished. You lose her as easily as you lose a button!

9   Lucie's hut

Jean   Half an hour's walk east of the village brings you to a stone column on top of which stands a small statue of the Madonna. Around the next corner, sitting on a bend in the road, sheltered under a precipice, is the house in which the Cocadrille lived her second life.

He stands outside her hut. The table is its door. He knocks.

Lucie   You're too late.

Jean   I have come to fetch my haversack.

Lucie   At this hour!

Jean   Excuse me. I'll wait in the road.

The table goes back to reveal her.

Lucie   All right, I'll pay you a coffee.

He goes in and sits. She cuts newspaper with a knife. The sound of chickens picking around the hut. The others, a chorus of the dead, listen at **Lucie***'s door.*

Jean   What are you doing?

Lucie   Something to wipe my arse with! Take your glasses off, they make you look like a priest. The last visitor I had was the priest. That was three years ago. In July 1964. It was the last priest, not this one. I could hear him coming for miles, wheezing and coughing. He asked for a glass of water but I knew what he needed – some gnole.

A chicken wearing a priest's biretta has settled on a chair behind her.

Cock   You are a child of the earth, Lucie.

Lucie   He said. Without land, I said.

Cock   You have things to be grateful for.

Lucie   Like this house you mean. Oh yes. Everybody whispers in the village that I don't pay rent for it. But look what a shack it is. It was built for one man and a horse. It was built for the roadmender. I'm the first woman who ever slept in this house. Name me another woman, I said, who would live up here.

Cock   None of them is a child of the earth, Lucie.

Lucie   I will show you one day what I am. I'm going to surprise you all. Father, I believe in happiness. (*She shoos away the* **Cock**.) That was the last visitor I had.

Jean   Three years ago.

Lucie   Where do you live?

Jean   In my mother's house in the village. I bought it from my brothers with money when I had it.

Lucie   So you have money?

Jean   I didn't make the fortune I dreamed of . . .

Lucie   That's obvious.

Jean   I was unlucky. Do you always sit in the dark?

Lucie   What did you find in South America – electricity?

Jean   A little more.

Lucie   What?

Jean   Enough to live on until they nail me in my coffin.

Lucie   So you've come back to die?

Jean   We're not young any more.

Lucie   I'm not ready to die yet.

Jean   Death doesn't ask if you are ready.

Lucie   If death comes to my door I'll tell him I'm not ready. I'm not ready!

The chorus of the dead at her door recoil a little. **Lucie** *chatters quickly and unintelligibly to herself. And stops, embarrassed.*

Were you unfaithful to your wife?

Jean (*standing*)   What a man does with his own skin is his own business. I'll take my haversack and I'll be going.

Lucie *fixes him with her look.* **Jean** *is made to sit down again.*

Lucie   All right, I'll heat the soup.

Jean   All right, then. I have a bottle of wine. (*Taking it from his haversack.*)

Lucie   So you thought you'd stay!

Jean   No. I bought it for myself at home. But we might as well have it now.

Lucie   After forty years that's all you have to show for it. One litre of red. (*To the stove.*) Did you hear that? He's come back a pauper. At least he's seen the world. (*To* **Jean**.) You

went round the world and I kept myself and here I am,
Jean. I kept myself together. Waiting. Forty years I kept
them off. Keeping myself, waiting. When you left and they
threw me into this hut of stones, I looked at my hands – you
can look at them, too.

Jean *stands and backs away down left where he sits to listen to her
story. The hut expands to fill the space.*

Lucie   Poor hands, I said, all your life you have worked
and what can you do now in this hut of stones?

The chorus raise the Madonna.

No land, no cow to milk, no pig to feed, no field to cut. I
looked at my hands and then I looked at the hands of the
Madonna – you know the one who stands on her column by
the road through the rocks – and they are the same hands,
Jean.

Lucie *has come centre to look.*

And I looked and I saw where her hands were pointing in
the grass at my feet, and there was a morille. And another.
And another. A bed full of mushrooms. I picked and picked
and put them in my skirt. In no time I had two kilos in
there.

The Madonna disappears.

Too many for any plate of mine. And I heard Father
saying –

Marius *appears from behind the table.*

Marius   Lucie, in the city you can buy anything if you
have money. In the city money breeds. Buy, sell, buy, sell,
buy, sell. And it makes little money and when little money
gets big and fat you kill it. In the city you can make money
with nothing. (*He spits.*)

Lucie   Yes, Papa. So I went to the city. With my skirt full
of mushrooms. I took the train, I crossed the frontier, I

walked for three hours and I thought, I can make 2000 with
a skirt full of mushrooms. And then I saw the prices.

*The chorus come forward as market traders, shouting their wares,
competing.*

7000 for one kilo! 7000! Yes, Papa, in the city money
breeds.

The chorus retreat and fade.

All around me people were buying and selling and I was just
sitting and waiting. Waiting for people to buy my
mushrooms. But nobody bought. And then at twelve
everyone started to pack up had leave. I hadn't sold
anything. I hadn't opened my mouth. In the city you have
to know what they want and how to sell it. Cèpes! Morilles!
Bluettes! Pigs' feet. Ox tongues. Monks' noses. Wolves' balls.
Death's trumpets – all the mushrooms, Jean. I still know
where a mushroom is waiting like a bitch on heat for a dog.
And if they want raspberries, I pick the wild raspberries. In
the autumn it's the blackberries. In the summer it's the
blueberries. And then the redberries, the huckleberries, the
juniper berries, the gooseberries, the bilberries and the
whatever berries. (*Going back to her table down right.*) And at
Christmas, for a bunch of mistletoe, I even get 5000.

Sound of a car passing, the headlights shine into her face. **Lucie** *raises
her fist and swears at it.*

They never stop. In the winter when they go past, I think of
shooting the driver. Why not! In the winter it's only the
three of us. The two needles and me. (*She finds them behind
her.*) But we work together. We knit little ski caps, gloves,
and baby boots. But we have to know who to knit for. If we
sell them in the market we get 2000. If we go to the wool
shop we get 3500. You have to know where to sell. Next to
the wool shop there's a shop window full of wood. Old
wood. Things we have in our barns – our hayforks, sledges,
cradles, milking stools . . .

Jean   Antiques, I think they call them.

Lucie   Antique, antique! I went in this antique shop once
and I said, if a stool costs that much, how much would I
cost? I could sell myself, piece by piece. 20,000 for a milking
hand. Double that for an arm. And how much would you
give, I asked, for a real peasant woman's arsehole? It's still
working, this one, even if it is an antique! In the city you can
make money with nothing.

She goes to **Jean**.

Do you still drink gnole? (*She pours him some.*) You know how
much I sell a bottle of this for? Eh? Eh? 9000. Don't think
me a fool, Jean – I found out about Marlboro. Marlboro.
2000 in the city.

She crosses the frontier, made by the **Customs Officer**.

Customs Officer   Anything to declare, grandma?

Lucie   Down to there, nothing – but underneath is a
present for any young man who wants it! (*Lifts up her skirt and
reveals packets of cigarettes. To* **Jean**.) I sell them for 3000 this
side of the frontier. I'm a smuggler!

*She goes back to her table where she picks up her bag and hat to go
shopping.*

Yes, everything in the city is hidden. Everything is arranged
in private. Private cars, private houses, private restaurants.
It took me two years to find my way around and even after
two years there were things I didn't know. One day it was
raining and I was caught in a crowd. I found myself pushed
into a huge shop. I'd never been in this shop. How did I
miss such a big one? I said to myself. And there I was,
standing in front of a lift. Émile! If only you could see me
now!

Lift Operator   Chocolate, coffee, teas, patisseries.
Madam?

*She sits in a café. The chorus of the dead are the other customers. Two
men meet and talk behind, and a man and a woman to her left.* **Lucie**
is served tea.

Lucie   For eighteen years that was the only day of the
week I sat in company. (*She smokes. She imitates the laughter of
the woman at the next table.*) Me with my Marlboro and them
with their new shoes. This is what money can do.

The man and woman get up to leave. **Lucie** *stops the woman.*

Hey. If you have enough money you can stand on your
head stark naked.

She laughs. The man puts a coin in her cup. She spits.

I have enough. I have enough.

*She wraps her small box-table into the cloth and takes it back to the
table in the hut as if it were her savings. Café fades.*

I have enough. I brought back money. And money saves
you. Money keeps you. I kept myself. You're a pauper, Jean.
Not me. My savings talk to me. When I'm soaked in the
forest, they say:

The dead advance and speak to her like her savings.

Savings   One day, Lucie, you'll be warm and dry.

Lucie   When my back feels broken, they say:

Savings   One day you'll have an armchair.

Lucie   And when I'm sick of talking to myself, they say:

Savings   One day, Lucie, you'll move back into the
village.

Chorus   The village, the village . . .

Lucie   That's what my savings say. Why don't you say
something? What did you lose on your travels – your
tongue? Why don't you say something, Jean?

Jean   Haven't your brothers, Henri and Edmond, ever
visited you?

Lucie   I saw the last of them the same night they brought
my furniture up here. They were ashamed to be seen

moving their sister up here in the daylight. My own brothers, fed on the same mother's milk, left me up here in the dark one night. Each month they were meant to pay me. Pay my arse! I watched them go through that window there. I followed them as far as the Madonna.

Chorus raise the Madonna.

There was a long white cloud in the shape of a fish. And where the fish's eye should have been was the moon. (**Lucie** *prays to the Madonna.*) Papa. Maman. You should have known your sons better. You always thought of them as they were when they were in the cradle. Shit! You didn't know where their evil came from. You died, Papa, not knowing that to make a child you need a woman, a man and the devil. That's why it's so tempting. (*She sees her mother and father.*) Papa, Maman. Go on, Papa, rut into Maman. Maman, pull him down! Go on, Papa, rut into Maman. When you were alive, you didn't do it enough, did you? You were always too tired and your back felt too broken. I give you my blessing. You have nothing left here. (*She turns to the Madonna again.*) If you stopped and saw me, you'd suffer. I'm not going to let you suffer, Papa, I'm not going to let you suffer, Maman, because I'm going to survive. I swear it. I'm not going to let you suffer. I'm going to survive. (*Going back to her table.*) And I have survived. My savings get me out of bed every morning before sunrise.

Chorus follow her.

They remind me when my dress is wet with dew that it will dry in an hour.

Crack of a bamboo whip behind her.

They tell me not to complain when I'm hungry because I'll eat later. (*The whip.*) And when my back aches and my shoulders are sore and my knees give me so much pain they make me cry out, (*the whip*) they remind me that one day I will buy a new bed and that I will move back into the village. (*The whip cracks again.*)

Jean   Why are you telling me all this?

Lucie   Wait.

She goes to the back of her hut. **Jean** *goes back to her table and sits.*
The hut shrinks to its former size. Then **Lucie** *returns standing on*
top of her hut in her wedding dress and veil. **Jean** *becomes conscious of*
her behind him and turns to look.

Jean   In God's name, what do you think you're doing!

Lucie   The last time we were together I undressed. My
poor Jean! You're shitting in your pants! I want to move
back into the village. You have a house in the village and
you haven't much else. I'm prepared to buy now a share of
your house until I'm dead, and I will pay you straightaway
in cash. The rest of my savings I'm keeping for myself. Does
that interest you?

Jean   The house is too small. The way you live is not the
way I could live. At my age I'm not going to change.

Lucie   I can change.

Jean   Why don't you rent a whole house to yourself? Have
you asked anyone else to take you in?

Lucie   Only *you* know me!

Jean   What you really want, what you have always
wanted, is for me to marry you!

Lucie   Yes. In church, with this veil.

Jean   You are out of your mind.

Lucie *comes down the ladder.*

Lucie   There's no one to stop you this time. You are
alone.

She touches his hand.

Jean   I can't marry you.

Lucie   Jean!

Jean   Again she said my name as she had said it forty years before and again it separated me, marked me out from all other men. In the pause between her twice saying my name in the same way, I saw myself as the young boy I had once been, encouraged by Masson to believe that I was more than usually intelligent; I saw myself as a young man without prospects, because I was the youngest, but with great ambitions; I saw my first departure for Paris which so impressed me as the centre, the capital of the globe, that I was determined to take one of the roads from L'Étoile across the world; I saw the last goodbyes to my family, my mother imploring me not to go all the time that I harnessed the horse and my father put my bag in the cart. America is the Land of the Dead, she said. I saw myself on the boat on which each day I dreamed of how I would return to the village, honoured and rich with presents for my mother. I saw myself on the quayside where I did not understand a single word of what was being said, and the great boulevards and the obelisk, the grandeur of the packing plants which I tried to describe in a letter to my father, for whom the selling of one cow for meat was the subject of a month's discussion. I saw the letter with the news of my father's death, I heard the noise of the trains through the window of the room where I lodged for five years, the epidemic in the shanty town and the carts bearing away the putrid bodies. Oh, the land of straight railways so flat and going on for ever; I saw myself in the train going south to Rio Gallegos in Patagonia, sheep-shearing and a wind that, like my homesickness, never stopped. I saw my wedding in Mar del Plata with all seventy-five members of Ursula's family. I saw the birth of my boys and my fight with Ursula to christen Basil 'Basil'. I saw the failure of my marriage, my flight to Montreal, the boys learning English, a language which I could never speak, the buying of my bar, the news of Ursula's death, the news of my mother's death, the fire in the bar, the police investigations, my Sundays in the forest. I saw myself working for years as a night-watchman, the buying of my ticket home . . . I saw forty whole years compressed within the pause. I looked at her wrinkled cider-apple face and I hated her. She made me see my life as wasted. Yet I was forced for the first and last time in this life to speak to her tenderly. (*To* **Lucie**.) Give me time to think, Lucie.

Lucie   Come and tell me when you want to, Jean.

Jean *leaves the hut. The hut dissolves. The table goes down.*

Jean   Before I could give her my considered answer, she was dead.

Lucie *is lifted above the table, blood steaming from her wedding veil. She is dumped in her bathtub coffin which is slid under her. The funeral procession begins.*

Jean   Her body was discovered by the postman who noticed that the window on to the road was broken and swinging on its hinges. She had been felled with an axe. The blade had split her skull. The signs were that she had put up a struggle. Her money, her two million, was never found. When I saw six, I still remember my father saying to me, 'Hey, Jean, when you let the cows out today, keep Fougère behind – she's going to the abattoir.' I remember him taking her bell and her collar and hanging them on a hook by the door and then he turned to her and said, 'My poor cuckoo, you'll never again spend a summer in the alpage.'

10   Lucie's funeral

Jean (*continued*)   Her death was a kind of disgrace for the village. There were fewer than fifty people at her funeral. There were many flowers on the coffin and the large unsigned wreath I had ordered was not immediately remarkable.

Lucie *sits up in her coffin.*

Lucie   Do you want me to say who did it?

The Street of Crocodiles

The Street of Crocodiles

The Street of Crocodiles

The Street of Crocodiles

The Street of Crocodiles

The Street of Crocodiles

The Three Lives of Lucie Cabrol

The Three Lives of Lucie Cabrol

The Three Lives of Lucie Cabrol

The Three Lives of Lucie Cabrol

The Three Lives of Lucie Cabrol

Mnemonic

Mnemonic

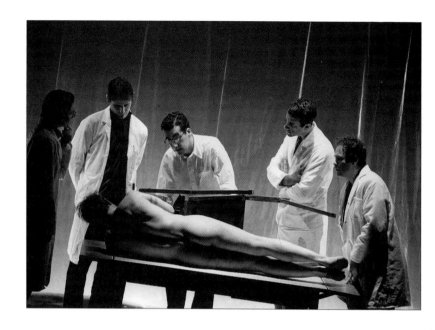

Mnemonic

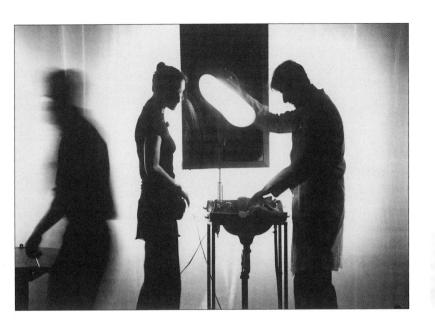

Mnemonic

Mnemonic

Jean   Did what?

Lucie   With the axe. He's among you, he's here in the cemetery, the thief.

Jean   You mean the murderer.

Lucie   It's the thief whom I cannot forgive!

Jean   It wasn't me.

Lucie   You thought of killing me. My brothers look solemn and hopeful, don't they? Solemn and hopeful! Did you decide not to marry me?

Jean   I hadn't decided.

Lucie   Then I'll wait till you've made up your mind.

The procession stops.

Jean   Lucie? Lucie.

They lower the bathtub and cross themselves. **Jean** *peers into the bathtub, trying to find* **Lucie**.

Lucie. Lucie, I . . .

He sits on a chair the chorus provide. The table is placed over the bathtub. A plate in front of him. His room.

She waited. She waited until Hallowe'en!

Lucie   I've learned something, Jean.

He starts and drops his spoon.

All over the world the dead drink on All Saints' Day. Everyone drinks, no one refuses.

Around the edges of the space, the chorus of the dead drink.

Every year it is the same, they drink until they're drunk. They know that they have to visit the living. And so they get drunk! On eau-de-vie!

Jean   You sound drunk now.

Lucie (*appearing from her coffin under the table*)   Why did you want to kill me?

Jean   You are drunk.

Lucie   I know why you thought of killing me.

Jean   If you know, why do you ask?

Lucie   I want to hear you say it.

She gets out of her coffin and stands in front of him. He can't see her and addresses himself to where he last heard her.

Jean   Yes, I thought of killing you the night you dressed up. Have you been to see the man who did kill you?

Lucie   It doesn't interest me.

Jean   You said you could never forgive the thief.

Lucie   I've changed my mind. I don't need my savings now. Why did you think of killing me?

Jean   Because . . . you were going to force me to marry you.

She drags her bathtub coffin from under the table.

Lucie   Force you! Force you! What with? (*Shaking it, she goes off up right.*) What with?

Jean   Lucie, wait! Well you were going to force me with your eyes.

11   Blueberry picking

Jean (*continued*)   She didn't come back that night, nor when I spoke to her the following night, not even the night after that. She didn't come back in the autumn, nor the winter, nor the following spring. Nor on St Lucie's day, her name day, the shortest day. At last the weather turned warm. My circulation improved. The apple trees blossomed, the potatoes were planted, the cows were put out to pasture in the alpage, the hay was cut. The next fine day, I told myself, I will climb up to the alpage, past Lucie's chalet, to pick some blueberries.

The dead support sloping plants to make the hillside. The sound of cicadas. **Jean** *picks.*

Jean   Though the day was hot, the mist hung below me, making the valley look like sea, and her chalet, long since deserted, was a shipwreck.

Lucie   Jean! Jean! How many have you picked?

Their voices echo in the mountains.

Jean   Half a bucket.

Lucie   As slow as ever!

Jean   I have calluses under my chin because all my life I have rested it on the handle of a shovel, doing nothing.

Lucie *laughs. The sound becomes the cry of a jackdaw.* **Jean** *looks for her but can't see her.*

Jean   Lucie! Lucie!

Lucie   Je-an!

He looks up. She is further up the slopes (the black wall), climbing quickly.

Jean   Lucie!

Lucie   Look, Jean, cherry stones in the birdshit. They fly with them all the way up here! Follow me.

Jean   Lucie! Wait for me.

He drops his bucket which clatters all the way down the mountainside, carried by one of the dead. He follows **Lucie** *up the slopes.* **Lucie** *leads him down the other side of the wall. The dead, forming the branches of the forest, help her down. He seems hindered by them, has to brush them aside. They go to the table, centre. She turns, revealed all in white and young again, and drops the other side and lies down.*

Lucie   Can you see me now?

Jean   Yes.

Lucie   How old am I?

Jean   You look twenty-five but you were born in 1900 so I suppose you must be sixty-eight. No, you were born in September so that makes you sixty-seven.

Lucie   I was born in the morning. My father was milking in the stable. White cloud-like smoke was blowing through the door. My mother had her sister and a neighbour with her. I was born very quickly.

Jean *lies beside her.*

Jean   You know everything about your life now.

Lucie   If I told you all that I know it would take sixty-seven years.

She gets up.

Come on, Jean.

Lucie *takes* **Jean** *by the hand and leads her downstage. The sound of hammering begins. Behind them the dead are building.*

12   Building the chalet

Jean   Where are we?

Lucie   This is where I am going to build.

Jean   Who does it belong to?

Lucie   Me. The dead own everything. I have land now. Land but no seasons.

Worker   Lucie!

As they turn to face the builders, **Marius** *comes towards them.*

Marius   Fifteen spruces for the columns, a dozen for the purlins, forty twenty-year-old trees for the rafters.

Jean   Marius!

Marius   I forget how many for the planks. We cut them all down when the axe entered her head. She told us afterwards she heard us sawing in the forest.

Lucie   That's when I brought them cheese and cider.

Armand (*dead*)   We were hungry!

Marius *introduces the workers.*

Marius   You remember Armand. He starved to death in 1924.

Armand   The granaries of the world belong to the dead, Jean.

Marius   Georges, who electrocuted himself because he knew he'd become a pauper.

Georges   I didn't mean to disturb anyone. I hitched myself up to a high-tension cable. When I died all the lights in the village went out.

Marius   Joset who was lost in an avalanche.

Joset   That was a great death.

Marius   And Mathieu who was struck by lighting.

Mathieu *waves.*

Jean   Why are they all here?

Lucie   They've come to help us.

Jean   Why only –

Lucie   Only what, Jean?

Jean   The ones who died violently.

Lucie   There are not so many who die in their beds. It's a poor country.

Jean   So am I to die violently?

She kisses him.

Lucie   So my contraband, I've smuggled you here.

Jean   Who are you building the chalet for?

Marius   You are warmer in bed with a wife, Jean. The whole war I thought of nothing else, I thought only of caressing La Mélanie in bed. There were some who had intercourse with donkeys, it never interested me, a beast isn't soft enough. When at last I came home I took her to bed and we had our fourth child. Even when I was old and lost my warmth, I thought of going to bed when I was working alone in the fields and sometimes thinking about it made me warm. It was my idea of happiness, you'll see for yourself, if you don't see now – it's better than sleeping alone.

Jean   But me and the Cocadrille –

Marius   The Cocadrille? It's now she's at the marrying age. Why else would I be building a chalet for her?

Jean   You were never a master builder and sixty-seven is no marrying age!

Marius   We can become anything. That's why injustice is impossible here. There may be the accident of birth but there is no accident of death. Nothing forces us to stay what we were. The Cocadrille could be seventeen, tall, with wide hips and with breasts you couldn't take your eyes off – only then you wouldn't know her as the Cocadrille, would you? You see all these men here. They have married her!

Jean   Not Georges!

Marius   Georges was the first. He married her the day after her funeral. The bridesmaids took the flowers from the grave. Those who die violently fall into each other's arms.

Jean   So I am to die violently.

Marius   Do you want to marry her? Do you want to marry her?

Worker   Everything's ready!

Marius   Let's raise the main beam.

Worker   The beam for the roof. The roof for the house.

Jean's *moment of decision. He takes of his jacket and goes to help the workers build. They cheer. They get ready to raise the central support of the chalet, which lies on the floor.* **Mathieu** *assigns everyone a position. All kneel and wrap their arms around the beam.*

Marius   The house for the marriage . . . You cradle the wood like you'd cradle a baby. (*He encourages them.*) Tchee tchee hissss. Tchee tchee hissss. Tchee tchee hissss.

Jean   I thought the dead rested after a lifetime's work.

They lift.

Worker   When they remember their past, they work – what else should they do?

Marius   Put your forearm under it. Tchee tchee hissss. Tchee tchee hissss.

The beam is lifted.

Get your shoulder under it. Tchee tchee hissss. Tchee tchee hissss.

They support the beam on their shoulders. Pause.

Jean   Yes, I should have married her.

They continue lifting.

Marius   Tchee tchee hissss. Quick, get the pole. Put the pole under it. Tchee tchee hissss.

Mathieu *puts a support pole behind the beam which is almost upright now. The workers groan with the effort and hold the beam for one last time as it goes into position. It drops into its hole on their last shout.* **Lucie** *appears.*

Jean   I will marry you.

Cheers. Chairs are brought. **Lucie** *and* **Jean** *sit.*

Marius *comes to them with the bouquet.*

Marius   Do you want to nail the bouquet?

Jean   Yes, I will nail the bouquet.

Jean *climbs the ladder placed against the beam.* **Lucie** *follows him. She sings. The dead join in.*

Lucie
   Apricagot de lee nay-a
   Sopiyay-a, *etc.*

Jean *reaches the top of the beam. There is a man the other side.*

Jean   Who are you?

Man   Lucie knew me as St Just.

Jean   You were in the Maquis!

St Just   We were ordered to dig our graves and then we were shot.

Jean   I will tell you something. After the Liberation, there were Nazis who escaped and came to the Argentine, and there they lived off the fat of the pampas.

St Just   They only escaped for a moment.

Jean   How can you be so sure?

St Just   Justice will be done.

Jean   When?

St Just   When the living know what the dead suffered.

Jean *nails the bouquet to the top of the beam.* **Lucie** *turns.*

Lucie   Wait for me.

She goes down slowly and goes off. All watch. The dead sing. But their singing is distorted and weak. They seem to be fading. Light fades.

Jean *tries to make out where* **Lucie** *is. He is frightened. Suddenly, the ladder disappears from under him. The tile shingles on the back wall begin to fall.*

Jean   Lucie! Lucie!

More shingles fall. **Jean** *clings to the beam as he falls. Everything collapses around him. Darkness. As he hits the floor and rolls, the black wall, a skeleton of wooden struts now, falls forward slowly and comes to rest on the two smaller beams left and right.*

Epilogue

Jean *goes to the stove right and sits.*

Jean   Before I was six, perhaps I was only two or three, I used to watch my father in the kitchen on winter mornings, when it was still as dark as night. He kneeled by this iron beast, feeding it. Now when I light the stove in the morning, I say to myself: I and the fire are the only living things in the house; my father, mother, brothers, sisters, the horses, cows, rabbits, chickens, all have gone. And Lucie Cabrol is dead. I say this, and I do not altogether believe it. Sometimes it seems to me that I am nearing the edge of the forest. I will never again be sixteen. If I am to leave the forest, it will be on the far side. But there are moments when I see something different.

The dead appear and lower the central beam so it rests like the others against the fallen back wall, making the slope of a roof.

Moments when a blue sky reminds me of Lucie Cabrol.

Blue backlight throws the roof into relief.

Then I see again the roof which we raised, built from the trees. And then I am convinced that when I leave the forest I will leave it with the love of the Cocadrille.

Music. Fade.

Mnemonic

*Dedicated to the memory of Katrin Cartlidge (15 May 1961 –
7 September 2002), our friend and colleague, who created and originally
played the role of Alice in* Mnemonic.

Mnemonic, originally a co-production with the Salzburg Festival, opened in July 1999 at the Lawrence Batley Theatre, Huddersfield, then toured to Cambridge Corn Exchange, Newcastle Playhouse, Oxford Playhouse, Salzburg Festival and Riverside Studios London.

A revival in 2001 opened at the Lyttleton Royal National Theatre, London and toured to Mercat de los Flores, Barcelona; Bobigny MC93, Paris; and the New York off-Broadway season at the John Jay College Theater.

In 2002 a second revival toured to Bosnian National Theatre, Sarajevo; National Theatre of Northern Greece, Thessaloniki; Munich Kammerspiele; Dramatyczny Theatre, Warsaw; Helsinki Kansallisteatteri; Theatre National Populaire Lyon-Villeurbanne; Bobigny MC93, Paris. The version in this collection was performed at the London Riverside Studios in January 2003.

1999 production

Conceived & Directed by Simon McBurney
Devised by The Company
Designer Michael Levine
Lighting Paul Anderson
Sound Christopher Shutt
Costume Christina Cunningham

Original Company

Cast Katrin Cartlidge, Richard Katz, Simon McBurney, Tim McMullan, Stefan Metz, Kostas Philippoglou, Catherine Schaub Abkarian

2001 Revival

Cast Katrin Cartlidge, Richard Katz (Eric Mallett in New York), Simon McBurney, Tim McMullan, Daniel Wahl, Kostas Philippoglou, Catherine Schaub Abkarian

2002–3 Revival

Cast Hannes Flaschberger, Dan Fredenburgh, Susan Lynch, Stefan Metz, Simon McBurney, Tim McMullan, Aurelia Petit, Kostas Philippoglou

Awards

1999 The Critics Circle Award for Best New Play
2001 Time Out Live Award for Outstanding Achievement
2001 Syndicat Professionnel de la Critique Dramatique et Musicale, Grand Prix de la Critique for Best Foreign Play
2001 Lucille Lortel Award for Outstanding Achievement off Broadway for Best Lighting Design
2001 Lucille Lortel Award for Outstanding Achievement off Broadway for Best Sound Design
2001 Lucille Lortel Award for Outstanding Achievement off Broadway for Unique Theatrical Experience
2001 Drama Desk Award for Best Sound Design
2001 Drama Desk Award for Best Lighting Design
2001 Drama Desk Award for Unique Theatrical Experience
2002 Golden Mask Award, Festival Mess, Sarajevo

Thanks to all those who have contributed to the production over the years: Simon Abkarian, Annabel Arden, Anita Ashwick, Simon Auton, BAC, Frank Baumbauer, Lilo Baur, Paul Bennun, John Berger, Niall Black, Steven Canny, Annie Casteldine, Guy Chapman, Chris Chibnall, Anna Clayden, Sadie Cook, Perrine Desprogres, Judith Dimant, Patrick Donohue, Natasha Freedman, Gareth Fry, Bronagh Gallagher, Kate Higginbottom, Paul Hollingbery, Rodger Hulley, Renata Klett, Sharon Kwan, Emma Laxton, Elena Lehmann, Michael Meller, Gordon Millar, Mitch Mitchell, Nicky Pallot, Lizzie Powell, Doug Rintoul, Christiane Schneider, South Tyrolean Museum of Archaeology, Kate Sparshatt, Dr Konrad Spindler, Polly Stokes, Professor Weir, Rod Wilson.

Note

From Scene Three onwards the Company remain on the stage throughout the performance. As the actors are already on stage, many of the characters' entrances and exits are not signalled in the stage directions. The cuts between the scenes are fast and fluid.

Scene One

An empty stage except for a chair and a stone DSC.

Director   Good evening, ladies and gentlemen. Before we begin I'd like to say a few words about memory. After the show yesterday somebody asked me, 'Why are you doing a show about memory?' and I was trying to remember . . . the origin of this show which is as much about origins as it is about memory. Maybe it is simply because they say that your memory starts to degenerate when you're twenty-eight and as I am now over forty the matter is becoming a little pressing. Or perhaps it is because one of the last great mysteries, this one we carry inside our heads. Why we remember, what we remember, and how we remember. How does the memory actually work? Is consciousness possible without memory? I don't think so. Not very long ago, in the middle of the last century, the twentieth century, people used to believe that individual memories were stored in individual brain cells. So to retrieve a memory all the brain had to do was to identify the relevant brain cell, get into it and . . . wham . . . out would come the memory. Exactly the same each time. Like an image on a hard disk in a computer. Call up the relevant folder, double-click on file, double-click again and . . . vlam! . . . the memory appears. My God how wonderful that would be. 'Darling, where did you leave the keys?' . . . vlam! . . . 'I left my keys in the left-hand pocket of my jacket which is on the chair to the right of the kitchen table.' Of course we know that's not true, it's certainly not true for me. 'Darling, where did you leave the keys?' 'I left the keys in my pocket . . . no, my trousers . . . in the kitchen . . . in the bed . . . in the fridge, where the fuck did I leave my keys?' That is much closer to how we experience memory, certainly my memory, it is fragmented, broken up.

And what we know now about the biochemistry of memory is that memory revolves around this idea of fragmentation. It is not so much the cells that are important in the act of memory, but the connections between the cells, this is where it really happens, the synapses, the synaptic connections. Here's a little computer graphic to help you understand that. And these connections are being made and remade. Constantly. And this process is called sprouting. Even as I am talking to you part of your brain is changing. You are literally making new connections between the neurons. They are being fabricated even as I speak. You get a little squirt of biochemical juice and sprout new connections. And this goes on through all of our lives. And these connections join up the fragments of memory, so if you like we can think of memory as a kind of map. But not a neat map like a map of a town. It's an unstable map like a weather map with highs and lows and wind and rain and so on, it is constantly changing. And each time we return to the map we find it has changed because of the new connections that we have made in the interim. So each time we remember we literally have to make a new memory, we have to create it for the first time, creativity is essential in the act of memory. In other words, the process of memory is almost exactly the same as the process of the imagination, it is an imaginative act.

For example, as I stand here trying to remember my text all sorts of other thoughts are coming into my head . . . for example, for some reason I'm thinking of my father. Why am I thinking about my father? I'll just follow that bit of the map. Probably it's to do with origins, this show being about origins, and he was interested in origins because he was an archaeologist. His origin, by the way, was that he was American. Well, everybody has problems. And my mother is Irish. That is not strictly true, she's part Irish, part Welsh. And a bit Scottish, and part English. Which I suppose makes me British. I'm British. But what is British? Buckingham Palace, Big Ben, fish and chips? Who knows? It's a question that fascinates me. On the way to the airport to fly here I was in a minicab. The driver had a very strong accent, so I asked him, 'For you, what is British?' And he said, 'I beg your pardon?' So I said, 'Well, I mean, where are you from?' and he said, 'London. Islington.' So I said,

'No, I mean before that, originally,' and he said, 'Germany.'
So I said, 'You don't have a German accent' and he said,
'I'm not, I'm Greek. But I have a British passport.'

And there you are . . . we started off with brain cells and
now here we are in Greece. Talking of which, the Greek
word for seahorse is *hippocampus*. Which would be
completely irrelevant were it not for the fact that this is the
name of the tiny gland, a chilli-pepper-sized gland, well
seahorse-sized actually, situated here at the base of the
brain. It squirts a little biochemical juice and then we
sprout. Squirt and sprout. And how does the hippocampus
help us to choose what we remember? Because of course we
don't remember everything. I'm told it chooses in two ways.
The first reason is that it fastens upon something we already
know. So we experience memory through familiarity. How
do we experience this? When we see something we know it
sets off a chain of memory. For instance, perhaps I thought
about my father because this was his chair. I *know* it. He sat
on it. And so did my grandfather. In fact it's a chair I know
very well because I've used it in another show. I have a
proclivity for using personal props in my shows. It was in a
show called *The Chairs* by Ionesco and there's another story
about that actually . . . but there we go, I'm re-routing
already, quick back on to the right map . . . the second
reason we choose to make memories is that the
hippocampus locks on to something when we get an
emotional shock. Which means we can imprint memories
very fast. For example, if I was to ask you what you were
doing on November the eleventh this year you probably
won't be able to remember, but if I were to ask you the
same thing about September the eleventh 2001 then it
comes back quite quickly. And the same is also true in
reverse so that when we are in an emotional state everything
can remind us of things; our memory works overtime. For
example, if anyone here in the audience, God forbid, has
had the experience of a lover having left them, for someone
else perhaps, you know that everything can remind you of
him or her. This stone. Ah, here she tripped, or this chair,

which is somehow a mnemonic for her whole body, here she
sat. Her legs, her back, her arms, her head, her breasts . . .
and so on . . . but you, for example, are unlikely to
remember that I have a stripy shirt on unless I attach it to
something. For example, if I give you a shock, if I shout at
you like this . . . you will get a little fright and therefore
remember the colour of my shirt *huh . . . stripy shirt . . . huh
. . . stripy shirt . . .* you see . . . *huh* gives you a shock, and you
squirt and sprout, squirt and sprout and you will remember
that I have a stripy shirt on . . . or perhaps you won't
remember anything. Perhaps there's no sprouting going on
in this audience at all. Yes, mnemonics are frequently
useless things. A spoon, perhaps, or a mark on a wall, a knot
in a handkerchief. Proust tasted a little madeline and he
remembered three volumes. A watch to remind us of the
time, a ring to remind us that we are married. And I have
this stone in my pocket to remind me not to go on for too
long. And a second stone to remind me . . . ummm . . . that
when . . . ah, yes, that I have a third stone in this pocket
which is there to remind me to tell you to turn off your
mobile phones. Anyone whose mobile phone goes off during
the performance will be ejected from the auditorium and a
letter will be written to your parents.

And now, ladies and gentlemen, all of this is leading me to
ask you to remember that when you came in to the theatre,
on the back of your chair you had a little plastic bag. Pick it
up, please. Open it and take out the contents. In it you will
find an eye mask and a leaf, such as you find on
transatlantic flights . . . the eye mask I mean, not the leaf.
And I know what you're thinking, you're thinking, 'Oh my
God, audience participation.' But it's all right. I'm not going
to make you put the mask on and spray you all with water.
I'm not going to rip off my clothes and rub my body in baby
oil and then squirm all over the front row, no, 1968 is a long
time ago . . . more's the pity. No, I want you simply to hold
the leaf in your hand and to put the blind on . . . your head
. . . Why? Well for this reason. Because before we offer you
some of our fragments, we want you to have the experience

of reassembling some fragments of your own, yours only. If anyone finds this frightening or they don't want to put the mask on, too bad – because it's going to go completely dark so you won't see anything anyway. Now, please, ladies and gentlemen, we would like you to put the mask on and hold the leaf in your hand and think back, to remember.

Blackout.

Think back to a time which is not really very long ago. Two hours ago. Where are you? Who are you with? Have you got your tickets yet? The memory of two hours ago probably comes back very quickly so now we will go further back. Two weeks ago today at exactly the same time. Now where are you? Who are you with? And what are you doing? Already that's probably more difficult, so we will go back to a time which is perhaps clearer in your imagination. New Year's Eve 1999. The turn of the millennium. Where are you? Are you inside or outside? Are you with friends? Can you remember what you thought the coming year would hold? And did it? Perhaps you can remember a little but not everything of that day, a few fragments. So now we will go further back. Eleven years ago. 1991. What can you remember that you did in 1991? Anything? Let's be more specific. Can you remember autumn 1991? September. Let me help you. It's just after the Gulf War and before Yugoslavia starts to split apart. What was the most important thing for you that year? Perhaps it's completely empty in your imagination, perhaps it rushes back because of a particular event, or there may be one or two fragments . . .

But now we will go even further back. Let's go to the first time you wanted to kiss someone. Who was it? And did you? And now our journey takes us even further back. We are going to when you are six years old. It's summer and you're standing outside. Look around you. What can you see? It might be your first day at school, or pre-school, primary school. Look down at your feet. What shoes are you wearing? Now, in your imagination, look up behind you, to your right-hand side and hold up your hand. A hand clasps

yours. It is your mother. Look up to your left. Another hand
clasps that one. It is your father. Your mother, your father
and you, standing together when you are six. And now look
back behind your right-hand side. Behind your mother, with
a hand on each of her shoulders, are her parents. Her
mother and her father. Your grandparents. And to the left,
on your father's shoulders, are his parents. His mother. His
father. Six people stand behind you. All looking at you. And
now look back again and behind your grandparents are
their parents. Eight great-grandparents, four grandparents,
your parents and you. And behind the eight of them are
sixteen others all looking at you. Now feel the leaf. It has
several veins. Imagine that each vein is a line of your
ancestry all coming down to you, the stalk. All of these veins
are leading to you. In one hundred years there are,
approximately, four generations. If you look back along the
line standing behind you, as you look back, at the beginning
of the nineteenth century standing in that line would be
256* of your ancestors, assuming that none of your family
are inter-related. At the beginning of the eighteenth century,
assuming there are no kinship ties, there is a line of 4064
people. At the beginning of the seventeenth century it would
contain approximately 64,000 and at the beginning of the
sixteenth, if you continue the same calculation, 1.5 million.
So a thousand years ago, if there really were no kinship ties,
that line would be longer than nearly all the people who
have ever lived. Which, of course, is not possible but it
means that you must be related to everyone sitting in this
theatre.

Lights up to reveal a man on stage. It is the **Director** *but he has
changed into the character* **Virgil***. He is still listening to the voice of
the* **Director***. The audience should be completely unaware of when
the change between live and recorded voice took place.* **Virgil** *has a
mask and is holding a leaf.*

* Following performances in New York and London, two members of the
audience wrote in to correct our figures to 254; 4,096; 65,000; 1 million.

Director (*VO*)   And now, ladies and gentlemen, gently, very gently, so that the light doesn't affect your eyes, take off your blindfold. Now look at the leaf that you have in your hands. Turn it over and look at the veins. Now you can see that from the stalk there are several other stalks, other veins. Imagine that each vein is a line of your ancestry. If you look closer still, there are even more stalks, interlocking, and tinier veins, branching and branching and branching, making more and more patterns (*SFX: a mobile phone starts to ring*) . . . in an infinite variety of ways, interconnections but repeating patterns . . .

Virgil *eventually realises that it is his phone. He answers. The other voice continues.*

Virgil   Hello. Whoever this is, I'm in the theatre.

Alice (*VO*)   Hi, Virge, it's me.

Virgil   Alice? Oh my God. Wait there. I'll go out.

He makes his way out of the theatre.

Director (*VO*)   . . . all the same patterns. A repeating pattern . . . a self-similar pattern.

Virgil   Listen, I'm going out, hang on . . . (*to imaginary audience*) sorry . . . sorry . . .

Director (*VO*)   The same pattern that is in this leaf is in your blood system which goes from your arteries to your veins, to your capillaries until the capillaries are no more than a cell wide.

Virgil   I'm only whispering because it's still going on . . .

Director (*VO*)   If you take a photograph of the delta of a river, from space, you find the same pattern, self-repeating patterns . . .

Virgil   I'm in the foyer now . . . Alice?

Alistair (*at the other end of the phone*)   I beg your pardon?

Virgil   What? Who's this?

Alistair   It's me. It's Alistair.

Virgil   Where's Alice?

Alistair   What?

Virgil   Where's Alice? Is she there?

Alistair   What do you mean?

Virgil   Alice phoned. Is she standing beside you?

Alistair   No, no. It's me. I just phoned you and now we're talking . . .

Virgil   You mean she isn't there? Is this some sort of joke?

Alistair   No, Alice isn't here. I wouldn't do that. Look, what's going on? What's that noise in the background? Where are you?

Virgil   Well I was in the theatre, in the middle of a show . . .

Alistair   You were in the theatre? What were you doing in the theatre for God's sake?

Virgil   I don't know. Why does anyone go to the theatre?

Alistair   Beats me. I'll call you later. Go back in.

Virgil   No, no, I can't, it's much too embarrassing, they told us to turn our mobile phones off and mine went off and . . .

Alistair   Naughty boy. What were you seeing?

Virgil   . . . well, it's very strange, I thought I was going to see some dance, or something avant-garde . . . it's this company that people said were really physical, apparently they used to be funny . . .

Alistair   Yes?

Virgil   But in fact this guy came on and started talking about the biochemistry of memory.

Alistair   It was probably a lecture.

Virgil   No, no . . . we were all given these little plastic bags with a leaf and a blindfold, I've still got mine on actually, and the whole audience was sitting there in the dark imagining our ancestors, like some kind of mass seance.

Alistair   You should be careful. You didn't have to sing any hymns did you? Maybe it was a religious . . .

Virgil   No, no. I tell you we were all thinking about out past. And everyone did it. And he said look down at your feet when you're six years old and think what shoes you're wearing and I saw those brown sandals with the little holes in the front. What were they called?

Alistair   Yes I had those . . . um . . . Startrite!

Virgil   Startrite! God, how did you remember that? But it was so strange. Actually, maybe that's why I heard Alice's voice. Something he said about connecting fragments. Listen, have you got a moment? I'd like to explain what he said.

Alistair   Why don't you come over for a drink? I'd love to see you.

Virgil   No, no. I mean now, before I forget it. He had a whole sequence of things.

Alistair   OK.

Virgil   Where are you?

Alistair   I'm in the garden.

Virgil   You're in the garden? Right, well, see if you can get hold of a leaf.

Alistair   OK.

Virgil   Have you got one?

Alistair   Yes.

Virgil   Right, now shut your eyes.

Alistair   Uh-uh.

Virgil   Now imagine that you are six years old. Reach up your left hand. Another hand takes hold of yours. It's your mother. And behind you on the right is your father. Your mother, your father and you. Now behind them are your grandparents.

Alistair   Yes.

Virgil   There's four of them.

Alistair   Yes.

Virgil   And behind them are your great-grandparents. Eight of them. And behind your great-grandparents are your great-great-grandparents. There are sixteen of them.

Virgil *turns to the audience. He is no longer talking on the phone. He is listening. As if he is remembering it. This effect is achieved once again by making an invisible join between the live telephone conversation and the recording.* **Virgil** *moves his chair, he is in a different space. He holds up the leaf as if recalling the conversation.*

Alistair (*VO*)   Blimey.

Virgil (*VO*)   So it makes a pattern coming down to you.

Alistair (*VO*)   It's beautiful.

Virgil (*VO*)   Right, now feel the leaf.

Alistair (*VO*)   Yes.

Virgil (*VO*)   Now the pattern on the leaf is chaotic.

Alistair (*VO*)   It's very rough.

Virgil (*VO*)   This is what he's getting at. The further back we go, the more chaotic our inter-relationships become. In other words, we do not know where we come from.

Virgil *suddenly starts to think about this again. He pulls out his mobile.*

Alistair (*VO*)   Yes. Yes. Look, could you just go over that again. I'm a bit lost.

Virgil (*VO*)   This pattern of our ancestry. This genetic pattern is the same as the pattern on the leaf. Do you get it?

Alistair (*VO*)   Oh, I see, the pattern on the leaf is the same as our ancestry?

Virgil (*VO*)   In other words, it's fractal.

Virgil *dials. We hear the phone ringing.*

Alistair (*VO*)   So the pattern on the leaf is a description of our ancestry?

Virgil (*VO*)   That's right, yes. Our ancestry is actually chaotic and interlinked just like the veins on a leaf.

Alistair (*VO*)   It's bizarre.

The phone is answered and the first conversation still continues in the background, as this new one begins.

Alistair   7226 5031.

Virgil   It's me again.

Alistair   Hello.

Virgil   I've just been remembering what we were talking about earlier and I wanted to ask you . . .

Alistair   Well, listen, could you remember it tomorrow? I'm just going to bed actually.

Virgil   What's the time?

Alistair   It's ten-thirty.

Virgil   God, you go to bed early.

Alistair   Well some of us have kids, they get up in the morning.

Virgil   Forget about your kids for a moment. I just wanted to explain it another way. I was just thinking, why did you phone me?

Alistair   I didn't. You phoned me.

Virgil   No, I meant earlier.

Alistair   Well I was talking to Sally and, you know, we're worried about you. Alice left such a long time ago and we think you should move on . . .

Virgil   No. That's not what I mean. You haven't called me for six months. Don't feel guilty, it's just that I want to know if you can remember the exact thing that made you think of me. Was there one thing? A spurt, that made you think about me?

Alistair   What like a trigger? Well, yes, I know what it was. I was sorting out some stuff and I found an old picture of you and Alice.

Virgil   That's incredible. Was it the one on the side of the mountain in Scotland . . .

Alistair   Yes, the one by the cairn.

Virgil   I don't believe it. I was thinking of that precise image the exact moment you called me. Do you see the connection?

Alistair   What, synchronicity?

Virgil   No. Chaos.

Alistair   Eh?

Virgil   Let me explain it another way. For example, why have I just lost my job?

Alistair   Well, they were going to get you sooner or later.

Virgil   No, no, why did I take that job in the first place?

Alistair   It's a complete mystery.

Virgil I'll tell you exactly why. It all came flooding back
to me. I suddenly had this image of the day I applied for the
job. What happened was that it was pissing with rain so I
stayed in bed for about an extra four or five hours. By the
time I got to the newsagent's they'd sold out of all
newspapers. So for some inexplicable reason I picked up a
copy of *Geology Today* . . .

Alistair So, it's all the fault of the weather?

Virgil Yes, in a way.

Alistair Seriously, if you're looking for one thing, like a
rainstorm, that set off a whole chain of events which
explains why your life's such a mess, you're not going to find
it. Life's not like that . . .

Virgil Listen, you live in a post-Einsteinian universe . . .

Alistair No I don't. I live in Teddington!

Virgil No, no, I'm saying it's chaos. You'd know that if
you ever read anything. But the thing is, in this mess of
unpredictability there are patterns . . .

Virgil*'s chair collapses.*

Virgil Fucking hell.

Alistair Hello, hello.

Virgil My fucking chair's just collapsed.

Alistair *laughs.*

Virgil It's not funny. It really hurt.

Alistair I'm sorry. I shouldn't laugh. I just wish I'd seen
it. Anyway, where are you?

Virgil Well . . . I'm at home.

Virgil *turns slowly on himself, mirroring the turning of his thoughts,
as his room, table, bed and sink assemble around him. A plastic curtain
creates a front wall. Noise of the street.* **Virgil** *looks out of the
window. We hear messages he has left for* **Alice***.*

Virgil (*VO*)   Hi, Alice. You didn't call me last night after the funeral. I hope everything went OK. I got your message but I haven't got a clue what it means.

Hi, it's me. It's coming up to six weeks now . . .

Hi, Alice. It's me again. Listen it's coming up to five months now since I heard anything so I can't go on with this. I'm not going to call again. Bye.

He ends up sitting downstage watching the television.

Television (*VO*)   If we look at a map of the weather system we see air pressures, isobars and winds. These maps look pretty but they're abstract. The normal state of the atmosphere is turbulence and the same is true of the settlement of the earth by human beings. Who can say what caused the Ethiopian drought, hurricane Tracey or the mass migrations which have peopled the earth. They are chaotic systems which frustrate every attempt at long-term forecast. Like the weather, humanity has always been in motion: migrating or in flight for the most diverse reasons in a violent or peaceful manner. A circulation that leads to perpetual turbulence.

Scene Two

Virgil *dials again.*

Alistair   Hello.

Virgil   Hi, it's me again.

Alistair   Oh God . . .

Virgil   I was just watching the TV and I suddenly realised something about Alice.

Alistair   Have you any idea what time it is?

Virgil   Um, no. I suddenly had this revelation about why she left nine months ago.

Alistair   It's two-thirty in the morning.

Virgil   Well never mind, I was awake anyway. Listen, you know I said that she had never said anything to me . . . it's like she dropped off the edge of the world.

Alistair   I'm whispering because I'm going out of the bedroom.

Virgil   Well that's not quite true . . .

Alistair   I'm sorry . . . I . . .

Virgil   Because she left me an answerphone message. Did I ever play it to you? No? Well listen to this. Let me play it to you.

The message plays.

Alice (*VO*)   Virge, you're not going to hear from me for a while. You have to wait now and this time you follow me.

Virgil   Did you hear that? Now listen to this and you'll understand.

He plays the video.

Television (*VO*)   Who can say what caused the Ethiopian drought, hurricane Tracey or the mass migrations which have peopled the earth.

Virgil   Do you see the connection between the two things?

Alistair   No. Would it help if I was holding a leaf?

Virgil   No, don't be facetious. This man is making a connection between the mass migration of people and turbulence. And I realised the same thing happens inside of us, turbulence. I mean, even something as simple as sleep, we know nothing about it. My doctor can tell me I've got insomnia but he doesn't know how or why.

Alistair   I don't have insomnia.

Virgil   Yes, yes, but the point is that Alice is in a state of turbulence. You can't wait and follow. She's contradicting herself. What's going on is that she's feeding back on herself. It's feedback, turbulence.

Alistair   Go to bed.

Virgil   Something must have happened to her. She's in a state of turbulence.

Alistair   Go to sleep, take a pill.

Virgil   And what is turbulence?

Alistair   Oh fuck off.

Virgil   Turbulence is fluid motion become random. Something must have set it off for her. So, yes, we live in a chaotic world. Yes, everything is unpredictable and, yes, we can be hurt in love but none of that matters. The only question about all of this unpredictability is, how do you live with it? Hello . . . hello . . . fuck you then.

Virgil *goes to the answer machine. The message repeats and repeats.*

Alice (*VO*)   Virge, you're not going to hear from me for a while. You have to wait now and this time you follow me.

His own messages start to come back to him. They merge with other fragments of the piece, a build-up of sound.

Virgil (*VO*)   Your answer machine again. I'm getting really worried.

Hi, it's me again. Listen, you've got to get on the end of a . . .

You've got to answer this thing.

It's me again, please . . . what's going on?

Right Alice. This is how I feel today. Fuck you. Fuck you.

White noise of mobiles going crazy. Loud music. Lies on bed. Tries a position to go to sleep.

Blackout. SFX: messages continue, 'Hi, this is Alice. Leave me a message.' Tries another position on the bed.

Blackout. SFX: messages continue, 'Please tell me what's going on.'
Tries another position on the floor against the bed.

Blackout. SFX: messages continue, 'Listen you've got to call me OK? I
don't mind just call me . . .' Tries another position on the table.

Blackout. SFX: messages continue, 'It's coming up to five months now
since I . . .' **Alice** *appears momentarily.*

Blackout. She has gone and only a chair remains. SFX: transposes into
loud wind, voices. **Virgil** *picks up the chair. It collapses in his arms.*
He takes his pillow and lies on the stone.

Scene Three

The wind increases. The company move on, slowly. They cross the
stage. The plastic curtain is drawn back.

Virgil (*VO*)   Who can say what caused a high-level
southerly air current between the fifth and eighth of March
1991 to transport a Saharan dust which darkened the sky
and fell over a wide area of the Austrian Alps colouring the
snow and the ice-fields a yellowish brown? It could have
been the movement of a camel, a mountaineer's sweat, a
man riding a bicycle. All movements of the earth contribute
to the chaotic movement of the weather.

They move in the wind.

Virgil (*VO*)   The Saharan dust meant that sunlight was no
longer reflected by the white snow fields. Instead, the dark
yellow layer absorbed the radiation and accelerated the
disappearance of the snow and the melting of the glaciers.

The others sit and we see **Helmut** *and* **Erika Simon**. *They are*
dressed in mountaineering clothing, standing on the bed and table as if
on the mountain top.

Helmut (*VO*)   From a distance of eight to ten metres, we
saw something brown sticking out of the ice. Our first
thought was that it was rubbish, perhaps even a doll,

because there is plenty of litter, even in the high mountains. But as we came closer Erika said, 'But it's a man.'

A camera flashes. They make their way to the body and stand still.

Erika *(VO)*   Ja, we thought it was a mountaineer who'd died there. We were shocked. We didn't touch the body. There was just a blue ski clip lying nearby and Helmut took a photograph as a record.

Helmut *(VO)*   There was an injury on the head and it looked like his arms were missing. He was lying face down in a pool of melted water.

Scene Four

We hear the sound of someone in a bath. **Virgil** *lies in a pool of light.*

Virgil *(VO)*   God, I was half asleep. What on earth are you looking at me for?

Alice *(VO)*   I like looking at you naked.

Virgil *(VO)*   Well I'm often naked.

Alice *(VO)*   But I like looking at you when you don't know I'm looking at you.

Virgil *(VO)*   Look, my skin's gone all wrinkly in the bath.

Alice *(VO)*   You look like an old man.

Virgil *(VO)*   Shut the fuck up. Pass me the towel. So what time is the funeral tomorrow?

Alice *(VO)*   Eleven o'clock.

Virgil *(VO)*   And what time are you leaving?

Alice *(VO)*   Nine-thirty.

Scene Five

SFX: train. The Eurostar train. **Alice** *is now listening to her messages.* **Virgil** *sits up violently as woken from a dream. He's looking at* **Alice** *as if what he sees is imagining or remembering.*

Telephone (*VO*)   Message received today at three forty-three p.m.

Virgil (*VO*)   Hi, Alice, it's me. Listen, you go to your mother's funeral and then leave me a message saying I'm supposed to wait months before you come back. OK, you telephone but what am I supposed to do with a telephone?

Telephone (*VO*)   To erase the message press three. Message erased. Message received fourteen December.

Virgil (*VO*)   Hi, Alice, me. Call me. Bye.

Telephone (*VO*)   Message erased.

Virgil *goes to the answer machine.*

Alice (*VO*)   Virge, you're not going to hear from me for a while. You have to wait now and this time you follow me.

Virgil *turns while a phone rings and the next scene begins. He is caught between worlds. It is the police station where they are registering the find of the body.*

Scene Six

Koler *answers the phone. His voice switches to pre-recorded half way through this speech.*

Koler   Polizei Imst, Koler . . . Was gibt's? A body. Yes, a dead body. A glacier corpse. It was found by climbers coming down from the Finailspitze. It was sticking out of the ice. No, we do not know who it is nor if it is a man or a woman. It could be a tourist but no one has been reported missing. The only record we have is of a man who

disappeared in 1941. He went into the mountains and was
never seen again. His name was Carlo Capsoni.

Virgil *moves back to the bed watching while* **Capsoni** *replaces him
lying on the rock.*

Capsoni (*VO*)   Carlo Capsoni was born on the eleventh of
November 1903 in Piacenza. The son of Giovanni and
Maraya Capsoni he was a music professor, a lover of the
pianoforte and an experienced mountaineer . . .

Capsoni *goes up into his room. A student (* **Virgil** *) enters and sits
down at the table as if it were a piano.*

Capsoni   Don't be frightened, as you were last week. It's
a piano not a rattlesnake.

Capsoni *gestures at a piece of music.*

Now from the beginning. Right hand only.

*The student begins the fugue but his fear means that he tortures the
music.* **Capsoni** *punctuates his attempts with cries of 'No, no!
Again.'*

Yes, well, we have a mountain to climb, you and I. But we
will get there, we will reach the Finailspitze and gaze
together across the universe. Only not just yet.

Capsoni *becomes increasingly frustrated.*

You can play this piece of music like an angel, I've heard
you do it. When we play a piece of music for another person
we often feel frightened, sick with fear, like a mountaineer
with vertigo.

Capsoni'*s tone softens.*

Why? Because we feel naked. And what does nakedness
remind us of? It reminds us that our fears are natural, that
we are all vulnerable. So let us agree that we are both
frightened . . .

*He sits on the table and we hear the sound as though he has sat on a
piano.*

. . . stark naked and that we climb this mountain together.
So from the beginning. With fear.

The student begins to play. This time the fear is vanishing.

That's it. Yes, yes.

The student is playing marvellously.

On the twenty-fifth of August 1941, Carlo Capsoni
ascended the Finailspitze having left word that he intended
to walk on his own to the Similaunhütte via the Schöne
Aussicht. He was never seen again.

Scene Seven

Virgil *mirrors the actions of* **Capsoni** *as he remembers climbing the
mountain. SFX: train.*

Koler (*VO*)   A music professor by name of Capsoni is still
missing, missing, missing. We still don't know who it is. We
don't even know if it is a man or a woman.

Alice *listens to her phone. She is behind the US mirror.* **Virgil** *sees
her momentarily and then collapses back on to the stone.*

Telephone   Message received fourteen December

Virgil (*VO*)   Alice, me again. Listen, what's going on?

Telephone   Message erased.

Scene Eight

*The wind is ear-splitting. SFXL helicopter. Two mountaineers signal
to a helicopter. They turn and approach the body.*

Virgil (*VO*)   Friday, twentieth of September 1991.

Koler (*VO*)   Sticking out of the ice was the sunburned
head, neck and shoulders of a man. On his back I saw black
lines. I thought maybe they were burn marks.

They begin to use a pneumatic chisel to free him from the ice. Loud drill noises.

Koler *(VO)*   He was not like other glacier corpses, this one didn't give off a smell.

They chisel some more.

The skin was just like leather.

Pirpamer *helps* **Koler** *to try and lift the body.*

Koler *(VO)*   We tried with the pneumatic chisel but it kept on slipping. Unfortunately, a couple of times it went right into his left thigh.

They cover the body with a plastic sheet.

No, we couldn't free him. It got so bad, the weather, we tried and tried but we couldn't get the body out of the ice. So we covered him as decently as we could.

Scene Nine

SFX: Eurostar train. **Alice** *takes her seat.*

Train *(VO)*   Ladies and gentlemen, in a few minutes we will be entering the Channel Tunnel; the crossing will take approximately twenty minutes. Mesdames et messieurs en quelques instants nous rentrons dans le tunnel sous la Manche. Cette traversée va durer vingt minutes. Merci.

Scene Ten

SFX: wind. A lone climber arrives to look at the body. He is an immigrant, a trainee cook.

Man *(VO)*   Saturday, twenty-first of September 1991.

He looks under the plastic. Shocked, he stands back.

Cook *(VO)*   Yes, there really is a dead man under there.

Scene Eleven

SFX: Eurostar, **Alice** *travelling.*

Train *(VO)*   Mesdames et messieurs, bienvenue en France.
Il est maintenant dix-sept dix heure locale. Ladies and
gentlemen, welcome to France. If you wish to set your
watches, the time is now five-ten p.m.

Alice *picks up her phone.*

Telephone   Message received fourteen December.

Virgil *(VO)*   Hi, it's me.

Virgil *sits up again remembering his own message to her.*

Listen, I quite understand you didn't want me to come to
your mother's funeral but it just would have been nice to see
you before you left. Where are you by the way?

Again she cuts him off.

Telephone   Message erased.

The vision fades as **Virgil** *stands up and puts his foot on the rock
DSC.*

Scene Twelve

The standing on the rock stimulates **Virgil***'s memory.*

Alice *(VO)*   Virge, read me that thing about funerals.

Virgil *(VO)*   Not again, Alice.

Alice *(VO)*   Please, just read it.

Virgil *(VO)*   OK. (*Reads.*) Nature has arranged matters so
that the bio-mass of every living creature is after death
reintegrated into the natural cycle by way of a very variable
food chain.

He goes to the sink to try and wash away the voices but they still continue.

Only man upset this sensible rule when he began to reflect on life after death, resulting in burials that sometimes raised the dead into the sky as in the towers of silence in Persia on whose platforms the dead are offered to the vultures . . .

He moves back to the rock. Behind him are two figures.

. . . sometimes burning them. Sometimes burying them in the ground. Sometimes preserving them for the life to come.

Virgil *moves back revealing* **Simonides** *and his sister* **Maria** *standing before the rock as if it is a grave. He sits on his bed listening to the scene as if he has heard it before. The space opens out as the light of an Athenian evening fills the stage.* **Simonides** *kisses his father's headstone and lights a cigarette. His sister crosses herself.*

Simonides   Hello, Father. Well, here we are 1973 and still I have no work. But never mind. How are you? Oh, you looked so beautiful when we buried you here in your new suit.

He breaks the cigarette in half and puts one half on the gravestone.

Father, this will be your last cigarette. I'm afraid you have to give up smoking now. Come on, have a puff. I'm leaving. I'm leaving Greece. There is no future for me here. I have to find it somewhere else. I was going to Germany to work for BMW. I passed the medical examination, everything, but in the end they didn't let me go. You know why? Because of you, Father. Because you fought as a partisan in the Second World War. For me you were always the mountain, for them just a communist. You have made me politically undesirable, Father. But, anyway, I found a solution. I bought a first-class ticket. I will travel to Germany first class. Nobody questions a rich man. The ticket was very expensive. I sold the house, I don't need it any more. Don't worry about Mama. She will stay with Maria. Yia sou patera.

Maria   Mi phygis Vassily. Mi phygis.

Simonides   De ginete mana, prepi.

Maria   Na xanarthis.

Simonides   Kala, tha dourne. Na tou pourne to tragoudi tou?

Mother   Ne.

They start to sing Rembatica, mournful. **Virgil** *returns to the rock as they retreat upstage. The room returns around him and he continues thinking about the previous conversation.*

Alice *(VO)*   I don't know.

Virgil *(VO)*   What?

Alice *(VO)*   What my mother would have wanted. I think I'd prefer to offer my body to the vultures. Read some more.

Virgil *(VO)*   It's a bit morbid.

Alice *(VO)*   I know, but I like it.

Virgil *(VO)*   OK. The practice of giving a human being a dignified funeral is so firmly rooted in the culture of almost all societies as to be hardly without exception.

Virgil *lies down on the rock again.*

Scene Thirteen

Crossfade to the mountain top. SFX: wind. A terrible wind. The whole company stand and gaze at **Virgil**'s *body. He has become the Iceman.*

Virgil *(VO)*   Monday, twenty-third of September 1991: the day of the official recovery.

One of the rescuers gazes out at the audience, the voice is clearly his.

Koler *(VO)*   I was with forensic expert Rainer Henn. We flew up to the Hauslabjoch to finally recover the body. (*Pause SFX: helicopter.*) It was so cold. (*Pause.*) We had no tools.

We were told the body was ready but overnight the body had once more frozen into the ice.

He organises the attempt to get the body out of the ice but it is a struggle. Using stones they try to chip it free.

They have criticised me a lot for the way the recovery was handled. These people have never been on a mountain at 3,200 metres under these conditions. It's very easy to sit in a centrally heated office.

Eventually they manage it and lift **Virgil***'s body, held stiff as though frozen solid, and gently deposit it in front of the table.*

We didn't do up the zip because by now the body was beginning to smell.

The mountain fades.

Finally we got the body out of the ice. It was a shocking sight.

Scene Fourteen

SFX: loud applause. DSL left there is a single spotlight on **Professor Spindler**. *He is speaking into a microphone, to a conference.*

Spindler   Thank you, thank you. People often ask me how I felt when I first saw him and you know it was such an incredible shock that I can remember every single detail. But of course when I realised who he was I had no idea how much or how quickly my life was going to change.

A telephone rings. **Koler** *lifts the body together with an assistant and positions it on the table, US. The scene shifts and* **Spindler** *is on the telephone.*

Henn *(VO)*   Professor Spindler. Good morning. This is Doctor Henn from the Institute of Forensic Medicine. Professor, would you like to see an untypical glacier corpse?

Spindler *(VO)*   Well, no, I'm an archaeologist. I'm not so interested in glacier corpses, they are too recent.

Henn *(VO)*   I don't think it's recent. It looks like a very unusual case. The police thought it was a music professor who died in 1941. Other people have speculated that it is from the nineteenth century or even the Middle Ages. But, professor, there is an object I would like you to see. It is a strange ice axe. It makes me think that it could be even earlier.

The light of the forensic laboratory fills the stage. **Scientists** *examine the body.* **Spindler** *is greeted by* **Professor Henn** *and inspects the body.*

Spindler *(VO)*   In front of me is the shrivelled corpse of a man. Naked except for a strange grass-filled shoe. Carlo Capsoni is definitely out of the running.

Spindler   This man is approximately four thousand years old . . .

The forensic scientists all speak at once, incredulous.

. . . and, if the dating is revised, he could be even earlier.

Virgil *sits up and moves off the table. He reaches under the bed and takes out the fragments of the chair, broken at the top of the show. These suggest the body of the Iceman.*

Virgil *(VO)*   So the man emerging out of the glacier was as a direct result of a sand storm in North Africa.

Scene Fifteen

The reverie is broken by the flash of photographers' bulbs. The forensic scientists have become **Journalists** *who stand around* **Spindler** *throwing questions at him, as if he were at the other end of a conference chamber, all shouting at once.* **Virgil** *holds the broken chair.*

(*VO*) We were crossing the border of the South Tyrol last fall, we reached the hut and the man there told us that somebody found a dead body . . .

All   Can we see the body, professor, can we see it?

SFX: music. **Virgil** *places the body on the table.* **Journalists** *again.*

Journalist 1   Herr Professor, was he murdered?

Journalist 4   Why is the body naked?

Journalist 3   I hear it hasn't got a dick.

Journalist 2   Is it a woman?

Spindler   Please, please, I'm not used to this. One question at a time, please.

Journalist 1   How do we know the body is four thousand years old?

Spindler   Thank you. Carbon dating which has put the age of the body back another thousand years.

Journalist 4   How long is that? Exactly how long?

Spindler   Think of the time between us and Socrates, then double it.

Journalist 3   Yes, but how long is that? Jesus Christ!

Spindler   Well, it's 3200 years before him.

Journalist 3   Before who?

Spindler   Jesus.

Journalist 3   Very funny, professor, cut the crap. When did he die?

Spindler   It's true. He died, as I said, 5200 years ago.

Journalists *slowly move SL of the table, facing* **Spindler** *moving to the other side.*

Alice (*VO*)   Is it for me?

Virgil (*VO*)   Do you like it?

Alice (*VO*)   I don't know. What's it for?

Virgil (*VO*)   Well, read the thing.

Alice (*VO*)   You read it.

Virgil (*VO*)   OK. Perhaps one of the most astonishing discoveries of modern times is the immensity of the past.

Journalists *again.*

Journalist 4   Professor, who was he?

Journalist 3   Where did he come from?

Spindler   Of course, we don't know who he was but we're hoping that investigation . . .

Journalist 2   What did he have with him?

Journalist 3   Any treasure? Silver? Gold?

Spindler   No, no silver, no gold. Please leave that alone. Don't touch the body. No, he had with him a broken stick, splinters of wood . . . Scraps of leather . . . Strips of hide . . . fragments.

Company freeze. **Virgil** *has picked up a pebble. Holding it stimulates his memory and the voices again.*

Virgil (*VO*)   This stone is called palaganite. It was thrown up on to the Canadian land mass twenty million years ago but it is much older than that. It is from the beginning. Palaganite is thought to be 400 million years old.

Alice (*VO*)   So that's the point, is it?

Virgil (*VO*)   Yes, what you have around your neck is . . .

Alice (*VO*)   . . . 400 million years old. Mmm.

Alice *disappears upstage, behind the mirror.* **Journalists** *again. They are SL, by the chairs, facing* **Spindler** *who is behind the bed.*

Journalist 3   I'm not being funny but what is so special about this body?

Spindler   The fact that he stepped to us directly out of his everyday life – that makes him one of the most valuable archaeological finds of the century.

Journalist 3   Right, so how much is he worth, then? Just give us a rough ball-park figure.

Spindler   I mean to say that this body is unique. His monetary value is irrelevant. In any case it is impossible to calculate.

Journalist 2   If he is so valuable, who does he belong to?

Spindler   That has yet to be determined.

Cut to **Virgil**'s *room.*

German (*VO*)   Hello, hello, this is Frau Schmidt speaking. I've just seen the Iceman on the television and I think he is my grandfather.

Journalists *stand up facing* **Spindler**, *who is still behind the bed. SFX.*

Journalist 1   Professor, what's the sex of the body?

Journalist 2   Yeah, tell us.

Journalist 3   Is it a woman or a man?

Spindler   His genitals are desiccated. They cannot be seen. But we have established beyond doubt that the body is definitely male.

SFX cut. Music.

Australian (*VO*)   Hello, this is Katie McIntyre from Sydney, Australia, g'day. I wondered if you could help me, I'm undergoing IVF treatment at the moment, is there any chance of some of that Neolithic sperm coming my way. Hello? Hello?

Journalists *again. Now they move downstage facing the audience, and* **Spindler** *is now upstage of the table.*

Journalist 1   Herr Professor, apparently he was found on the frontier?

Spindler   Yes.

Journalist 3   Which frontier?

Spindler   On the frontier between north and south Tyrol.

Journalist 3   In Austria?

Spindler   No, no, on the border between Austria and Italy.

Journalist 4   Yes, but which side of the border was he lying on?

Spindler   That is being looked into, we think possibly . . . Italy.

Journalist 2   So who does he belong to?

Spindler   At present, the University of Innsbruck.

Journalist 3   Which is where?

All   Austria.

Italian   But, professor, is he Austrian or Italian?

Spindler   Can we have another question about the body?

Italian   No, professor. Our police, the Italian police, are presently up at 3200 metres measuring the frontier. With rob.

Innsbruck   With rob?

Italian   Yes, rob!

Innsbruck   Who's Rob?

Italian *representative holds out a piece of rope.*

Italian   No, rob. Rob!

Innsbruck   Oh . . . rope, rope. Yes, well, our men are up there too.

Argument between **Journalists***, as they stretch out two pieces of elastic to create geometric shapes. VDX of the Alps, the Oetztal region.*

Spindler   No longer frozen, the body is sodden. No head hair, no body hair, no pubic hair. His chest and abdomen are sunken, and in the eye sockets his eyeballs are still recognisable.

Virgil (*VO*)   How many mourned him when he disappeared? He has gone to the mountain, is that what they said? How many songs did he know?

Italian   Tells us that the spot is on Italian territory by approximately three lengths.

All   Three lengths?

Italian   Three lengths of rope which is roughly 120 metres. Therefore he is Italian.

The **Journalists** *break out into an argument about ownership of the body.*

Innsbruck   Herr Professor, with all due respect, before 1919 this entire area, including the place where the body was found, belonged to Austria, to be precise the Austro-Hungarian empire. Would you care to comment.

SFX: loud camera clicks. Then silence.

Spindler   No.

SFX: montage of calls claiming a connection with the body, from Greece, Switzerland, France etc . . . they are fast cut with **Spindler***'s words.*

This man comes from a time before frontiers.

The protection of the body . . .

It is my belief that turning this pitiful bundle of humanity into a sideshow is not compatible with human dignity.

The noise cuts. **Spindler** *is projected on to the black plastic.*

I have just been given the permission by the relevant authorities to announce that, as from this moment, the body is officially an ancient monument.

Scene Sixteen

There is the sound of applause. A metal frame is held US of the table. The body has become a chair. The people gaze dispassionately through the window, rubbernecking the chair.

Virgil *(VO)*   Naked except for a strange grass-filled shoe.

The image is reversed. The frame is now DS. The people are looking US at the Iceman. **Spindler** *lectures, holding a microphone.* **Virgil** *crouches disconsolately on the bed. He turns towards the headboard as a video is projected on to his back. This is a live projection.*

Spindler   So the skin, which is now leathery and tough, changes colour across the body. If you look through the window of the refrigeration chamber, you can see that it changes from a pale ivory, through brown, to almost black. Now this refrigeration unit is kept strictly between zero and minus six degrees Celsius, and there is a degree of humidity which keeps it at the frozen conditions of the Hauslabjoch where he was found. If you'd like to come and look through from this side, you can see marks on the body. These marks are tattoos. The Iceman had fifty-seven tattoos across his body.

A pen draws the Iceman's tattoos live on the projection on **Virgil***'s chest.*

They are there because of pain. They are made by puncturing, scoring or cutting the skin with a very sharp instrument. A coloured paste, most likely a combination of charcoal and saliva, was then rubbed into the open wound. We know that they are there because of pain because X-rays of the bones adjacent to the tattoos show degenerative changes indicating that in those precise areas the Iceman was suffering from severe arthritis and rheumatism. Now if we look more closely at where the tattoos are concentrated on the backs of his legs and the lower lumber region of the spine, we can see that he could not have done them by himself to himself. This was part of an ongoing course of treatment administered by someone with the ability to heal, quite possibly someone from within his own community.

Scene Seventeen

Virgil's *mobile phone rings. He turns DS to answer it. The video image is now unclear.*

Virgil (*sleepy*)   Hello. Hello? Who is this? Hello.

Alice   It's me.

Long pause. **Alice**'s *face appears gradually on* **Virgil**'s *naked chest.*

Virgil   What? Who is this?

Long pause.

Alice   It's me, Virge. It's me. Please don't hang up.

Virgil   Alice.

Pause. They speak together.

If this is some kind of joke? . . . Who is this?

Alice   I know it's the middle of the night.

Virgil   What?

Alice   What? I said it's the middle of the night. I'm sorry.

Virgil   Alice?

Alice   Virge, I need to speak to you.

Virgil   Where are you?

Alice   How are you?

Virgil   What do you mean?

Alice   How are you?

Virgil   When did we last speak?

Alice   A couple of months ago. My mother's funeral.

Virgil   Alice, that was nine months ago. And by the way, we didn't speak. You just left a message on the answerphone.

Alice   I'm sorry, Virge. Please don't hang up. I need to talk to you. Something strange has happened.

Virgil   What?

Alice   I don't know where to begin.

Virgil   Why don't you begin by simply telling me why you've done what you've done?

Alice   Please, Virge, I'm trying to remember. It's difficult.

Virgil   Yes?

Alice   Please, Virge . . .

Virgil   It's OK, just tell me what happened.

Alice   I'm trying, it seems so long ago. After my mother's funeral, well her cremation . . .

Virgil   So no vultures, then?

Alice   What?

Virgil   It doesn't matter.

Alice   Well after her cremation I lost it. I remember I wanted to run, so I took that money from our account.

Virgil   Oh yes, the £2,500 . . .

Alice   I know, I know it was everything. I was . . .

Virgil   What?

Alice   Virge, please. Just listen. Try to listen.

Virgil   I am.

Alice   I lost it. I remember going to Waterloo station. I remember standing on the platform for hours. And then I got on a train to Paris.

Scene Eighteen

The video image freezes and disappears. SFX: train. It thunders through **Alice***'s voice and we are in the Eurostar train. She is looking out of the window.* **Virgil** *is still listening on his mobile.*

Alice (*VO*)   She told me my father was dead. She always told me my father was dead. The one time I asked her about the card which came for her every Christmas, the one time I asked her about it . . . she never said a thing.

Virgil   What did you do next?

Virgil *stands in the middle of his room.*

Alice (*VO*)   Changed in Paris and took a night train to Berlin.

Virgil   To Berlin? Berlin?

Virgil*'s room inverts. The chairs are carried SR across to where the bed is. The bed glides over* **Virgil***, who is now lying down, with* **Alice** *lying on it, as if on a couchette on its way to Berlin.*

Alice (*VO*)   She died. She never said a thing. Never said a thing.

It was at the funeral, there was a woman who told me my father was alive. Could be alive. Might be living. Somewhere.

The bed is still moving above **Virgil** *who lies beneath it.* **Alice** *in the sleeping compartment.*

He met my mother on the Baltic coast near Klaipeda, Lithuania. 1962. It was late summer. Late summer. Klaipeda, Lithuania.

Virgil (*VO*)   Lithuania.

Alice (*VO*)   . . . Lithuania. I'm Lithuanian.

I know nothing about him. I have nothing that belongs to him. All I have is a wind-up watch, Russian-made, which I found wrapped in yellowing paper at the bottom of one of my mother's study drawers. Broken.

Virgil (*VO*)   Broken.

Alice (*VO*)   Broken.

She lies down and goes to sleep.

Scene Nineteen

Spindler *and a group of* **Scientists**.

Spindler   A broken stick.

Scientist 3   A broken stick.

Scientist 2   Splinters of wood.

Scientist 1   Strips of leather.

Scientist 4   Fur.

Spindler   Tufts of twisted grass.

Scientist 4   Fragments of bark.

Scientist 1   Two round objects on a piece of twine.

Spindler *and* **Scientists** *examine objects on the mountainside.*

Spindler   A broken stick which was found here (*SFX: wind*) up on this ledge where the Iceman must have placed it or dropped it on his way down to the gully. We imagine he came this way to this rock because we found some of his equipment, which was made of birch bark, just here. Some of it was pulverised, possibly by those people who came to excavate the body. And we know that he came this way because this is where his head was. All of these objects were left exactly where he dropped them or placed them five thousand years ago when he came up here to this lonely place and lay down on his left and died.

Virgil *puts the mobile to his ear. SFX: screech of train wheels.*

Scene Twenty

Alice *(VO)*   Berlin.

She leaves the train and collides with a woman on the platform. Her bag falls and the woman helps her pick it up. They shake hands and part. **Virgil** *moves across the stage, on the phone.*

Virgil   Alice. What was that?

Alice *and the woman rewind into their original positions. They move forward again. The woman collides with her again. Same result. This happens exactly the same again. After this,* **Alice** *hurtles CS. The streets of Berlin form around her. She is accosted by a ranting* **East Berliner**.

East Berliner   Jetzt wo die Mauer weg ist, weiss ja keiner wo er hingehört. Jetzt kommen sie alle zurück, die Idioten, mit Geld in der Tasche, bauen sie uns Klotzen vor die Tür. Kuck dir doch nur mal den Potsdamer Platz an! Da kriegste ja keine Sonne mehr im Gesicht. Berlin, Berlin! Was ist denn das geworden? Lichtenberg . . . Köpenick, da kannte ich einen, dem seine Zähne haben sie ihm alle rausgeschlagen. Ja und ich? Wo soll ich denn jetzt hin. Ich bin doch hier geboren. Ist doch alles nur Scheisse jetzt, ist doch nur Scheisse . . .

Another man laughs hysterically. A woman begs. Men move their chairs around **Alice** *until they have created a café. She sits.*

Alice   Eine Kaffee, bitte.

She turns to look at the men beside her. They suddenly put homburgs on their heads.

Alice (*VO*)   Started looking at men over sixty in a different way. Was he ever on the Baltic coast?

The men remove their homburgs as she looks away. Waiter returns with the coffee, asking for payment. She can't find her purse. She searches desperately hoping that it isn't stolen.

Alice   Shit. Fuck, fuck.

Alice *looks up and remembers. We see again the moment when the woman stole it.*

Alice (*shouts*)   No.

She moves towards the bed. Cross-fade to the sound of a hotel room. **Virgil** *is sitting in the bed. She undresses and gets into bed. As she gets into it, he gets out. Their movements mirror one another. She looks at her father's watch.*

Scene Twenty-one

Virgil *shakes his head, disbelieving. He speaks into the phone.*

Virgil   All of it? I mean, what were you thinking?

Alice (*VO*)   I was thinking was he ever here, in Berlin or even on the Baltic coast?

Virgil   Jesus, Alice. I can't believe it. This whole story. You.

The scene cuts to the archaeological laboratory.

Spindler   Yew.

Scientist 1   Lime.

Scientist 2   Ash.

Scientist 3   Hazel.

Scientist 4   Birch.

Spindler   Norway spruce.

Scientist 1 Blackthorn.

Spindler The Iceman had seventeen different types of wood on or about his body when he died. Seventeen. The broken stick. One metre eighty-two in height.

Scientist 3 A bow.

Spindler And near it a quiver.

Virgil *is holding his mobile. By chance almost it forms the central strut of the shape of a bow the others form with their fragments of wood.*

Scientist 4 Arrows.

Spindler A Neolithic bow, had a force of up to forty kilograms. At fifty metres the arrow would pass straight through you.

The **Scientists** *form images with the fragments of wood, moving them like arrows.*

Spindler The wooden boards.

Scientist 1 A back pannier.

They form the shape of a back pannier on **Virgil***'s body.*

Spindler A wooden-framed back pannier still used in parts of Europe in the twentieth century. The fur.

Scientist 3 A hat.

Spindler The strips of leather.

Scientist 2 Leggings. Trousers.

Spindler The fit was loose, allowing movement to bend and climb. The scraps of hide.

Scientist 2 A pouch.

Spindler And in the pouch . . .

Scientist 2 Fire-lighting equipment.

Alice *sits up, pulls a cigarette from her bag and lights it.* **Virgil** *mirrors this in front of the TV DSR.*

Spindler   Matches. And the fragments of bark.

Scientist 4   Birch bark.

Scientist 1   A cylindrical container.

Spindler   A box.

Scientist 4   Blackish inside . . .

Spindler   Containing . . .

Scientist 4   Norway maple leaves and flakes of charcoal.

Spindler   This was a vessel for carrying live embers. And the two round objects on a piece of twine.

Scientist 1   Birch fungus.

Spindler   Five thousand years before the discovery of penicillin.

Scientist 1   A natural antibiotic.

Spindler   A travelling medicine kit.

Virgil (*VO*)   How many songs did he know?

Spindler   Seventeen different types of wood, seventeen. Each perfectly suited to their task.

Virgil (*VO*)   How did he imagine immortality? For imagine it he did.

Spindler   He was complete.

Virgil (*VO*)   How many children did he have?

Spindler   What was he doing?

Virgil *sitting by the TV speaks to* **Alice** *in his mobile.*

Virgil   Jesus, what did you think you were doing? Where did you think you were going?

Alice *in the bed turns in her sleep violently.*

Scene Twenty-two

A **Maid** *bangs on* **Alice***'s door. She doesn't wake. The* **Maid** *explodes into the room and speaking quickly and aggressively attempts to get her out of there.*

Maid   Aufmachen. Aufmachen, bitte.

Alice   Fünf minuten . . . bitte . . . fünf minuten . . .

Maid   Nein, ich habe keine fünf minuten. Sie müssen das zimmer bezalen.

Alice   Christ . . . ein . . . ein . . . entschuldigung.

Maid   Ja, ja, entschuldigung, entschuldigung, ich werde probleme haben. Stehen sie auf, auf jetzt . . . A mais elle est a poil en plus . . . .c'est dégueulasse.

The **Maid** *is trying to make the bed and clean the room.*

Alice   Ah, vous parlez français?

Maid   Oui.

Alice   Oui, je peux mieux m'expliquer en français. Ecoutez, je suis désolée. C'est un jour terrible pour moi, hier, on m'a volé tout mon argent . . .

Maid   C'est Berlin ici, madame: faut faire attention. Depuis que le mur est tombé C'est une vraie catastrophe. C'est plein d'étrangers! Il y a les Polonais, les Russes, les Juifs . . .

Alice   Oui et les Français aussi!

Maid   Quoi les Français? Je suis Allemande moi, madame!

Alice   Mais vous parlez très bien Français pour une Allemande.

Maid   Oh . . . c'est à dire je suis venue, je me suis mariée et puis . . . et puis de quoi je me mêle? Vous êtes de la police? Vous voulez voir mes papiers?

Alice   Non, non. Doucement, doucement. J'ai dit que je suis desolée, alors calme . . . .

The **Maid** *discovers her watch amongst the bedclothes.*

Maid   Je suis calme! C'est à vous ça?

The **Maid** *drops the watch on the floor. We cut immediately to a taxi.* **Alice** *picks up her watch, sits in the back of the car.*

Scene Twenty-three

Alice *is in the taxi. She's trying to get the watch to work. The driver,* **Simonides***, is in front.*

Simonides   Where are we going?

Alice   Waterloo, please. The Eurostar.

Simonides   Eurostar. Yes. Going to Paris?

Alice   Yes.

Simonides   That's great.

Alice (*shaking her watch*)   Shit.

Simonides   Are you talking to me?

Alice   No. Sorry. This watch, it's broken. I think it belonged to my father.

Simonides   Oh, do you want me to take a look?

Alice   No, no, it's very old. It's delicate.

Simonides   All right. Just a look to your watch. Trust me.

Alice   Do you know about watches?

Simonides   Yes, yes, I know everything about watches.

He pulls over, takes the watch.

I don't believe it.

Alice   Do you know where it's from?

Simonides Of course, it's a communist watch. From the Soviet Union.

Alice It's Russian.

Simonides Yes. It's wonderful. Very nice but not delicate at all. It needs only a regulation. I will fix it for you in one minute.

Alice Thank you very much.

Simonides You're welcome.

Alice Where are you from?

Simonides Me? I am from Islington.

Alice No, no . . . I mean originally.

Simonides Oh. I see what you mean. I am from Greece. There you go. It works now.

Alice Thank you.

Simonides You are very welcome. And you? Where are you from?

For a moment we see **Spindler**, *still in the midst of the investigation.*

Spindler He was travelling north.

Virgil *is now in the taxi.*

Simonides (*to* **Virgil**) And you? Where are you from?

Alice *gazes out.* **Virgil** *looks up. A moment of suspension.*

Scene Twenty-four

Cut back to the hotel room. **Alice** *grabs her watch from the floor and puts it to her ear.*

Alice Fuck! Oh, no!

Maid Merde!

Alice   It's stopped. Vous êtes une fucking stupid woman.

Maid   You speak English?

Alice   Yes, I speak English.

Maid   You are English!

Alice   No. I'm an Irish Lithuanian from North fucking London. Do you want to see my passport?

Maid   No, no.

Alice   Alors, c'est cassé! Oui. Cassé. Voilà!

Maid   Oh, merde, y'faut vraiment que ça m'arrive a moi ça!

She taps the watch on the headboard of the bed.

Alice   Don't do that! Give me the watch.

Maid   Please, you don't tell the manager!

Alice   I'm not going to tell the management.

Maid   But you promise because it's also your fault!

Alice   I'm not going to tell the management. Just give it back to me . . .

Maid   Because if I lose this job I'm back on the street.

Alice   It's important. Give it back.

Maid   Groß Berlin, big trouble . . .

Alice   It belonged to my father.

*We are back in **Simonides**'s taxi.*

Simonides   And to his father before him. My grandfather. Now they are mine. They are worry beads but personally I have no worries, they are just to kill the time. I'm going straight here, I think it's better, isn't it? You know, my worry beads are not Greek, they're Turkish. My grandfather was a Greek refugee from Turkey. He was speaking Turkish better than Greek, I speak Greek better than English and my son, he speaks English better than Greek. Here is my little boy. He looks like his mother but only the face because inside he's like me.

Back in the hotel room.

Maid   He gave it to you?

Alice   No.

Maid   Sorry. He's dead?

Alice   No, no, he's not dead. I'm looking for him.

Maid   Ah voilà. He left? Il a quitté vot' mère, c'est ça! Ah les hommes, c'est bien tous les mêmes!

Alice   No. It's more complicated than that.

Maid   Non, non, ce n'est pas compliqué. The men: one day they are here, then they disappear. It is like that. You know my husband . . .

Alice   It's not what you think.

Maid   Of course it's what I think. I'll show you something. This is my little girl. She looks exactly like her father. Only the face though because inside she's just like me, looking forward. You have to forget the past.

Alice   Thank you. I know what I'm doing.

Maid   Even in Berlin when you get your wallet stolen? How much money was in there? In the past we arrive always too late. Don't go back, go home.

Scene Twenty-five

*The **Scientists** examine the Iceman's objects. The detail of their work is picked out on a television screen and projected on to the pillows of the bed.*

Spindler   He was travelling north. Why? Because the glowing embers in his birch bark container were kept warm

by a layer of insulating leaves, leaves from the Norway
Maple which five thousand years ago grew only to the south
of where the Iceman was found. So he must have been
travelling north.

Scientist 1   The condition of the leaves is so good that
chlorophyll can still be extracted using alcohol.

Scientist 3   They are still green.

Spindler   Freshly picked.

Scientist 1   And on the leaves traces of corn. Recently
threshed.

Scientist 3   So he came from an agricultural community.

Spindler   They were not just hunter-gatherers.

Scientist 1   Analysis of the leaves tells us that for fuel he
used six different types of wood.

Spindler   They were taken all the way from the valley
floor in stages right up to the edge of the tree line.

Scientist 1   Analysis of his stomach contents show that his
last meal consisted of a small amount of goat and grain.
Traces of pollen in this last meal come from a spring
flowering shrub.

Scientist 2   So he died in the spring.

Spindler   While winter was still a threat. So a man leaves
his village carrying little or no food.

Scientist 1   He lights fires at different altitudes.

Scientist 3   As he climbs the mountain.

Scientist 1   He is travelling fast.

Spindler   He was an experienced mountaineer. Why
would he put himself in that position? He was travelling
north into the wilderness of the Alps with no food. What
was he doing?

Virgil *and* **Alice** *are on the telephone.*

Virgil   So, why didn't you?

Alice   What?

Virgil   For Christ's sake. Just do what she said. Come home.

Spindler   What was he doing . . .

Scene Twenty-six

An instant cut to a train crossing Central Europe where **Alice** *is talking with two* **American tourists** *and a* **Polish man**.

American   . . . in Minnesota . . . right after that moved on to Rapid City and so, now we live in Baltimore. I said to Trudi, we've moved dozens of times in our lives, for God's sake, now we've gotta make our journey to Europe. Here we are. We wanted to see if we could trace what happened . . .

Alice   Your roots?

American   Not exactly . . . anyway we prefer the train. Trudi's been really nervous of air travel since 9:11 . . .

Polish man   You American?

American   You want a cookie . . . ahh . . . wahlen sie einen biscuit? Sprechen sie Deutsch?

Polish man   Nie . . . Popolsku. (*He takes a biscuit.*) Thank you very much.

American   Yes, you're welcome buddy. (*Back to* **Alice**.) We've been in Europe for about three weeks now. We've seen just about everything. Paris, Rome, Berlin, Scotland. Scotland is such a beautiful place. So many happy memories from there. Hey, honey?

Trudi   Oh wow.

American   Mind you, Baltimore is a terrific place also, downtown you know they've completely renovated, there's nobody there any more, it's terrific . . . we live right outside . . . (*He carries on talking but is silent.*)

Alice (*VO*)   And so in Berlin my money was taken. Everything gone, everything except my passport. But I had to go on. Got a job in a bar in Bahnhofstrasse.

A brief image of a bar appears.

Went everyday to the office where you trace people, you know the branch of the police, what is it called? Der something something. Nobody knew where he was. But I found out there was a sister-in-law in Warsaw.

American   . . . The Warsaw ghetto. Trudi really liked the museum. I found it a little disturbing . . .

Alice   So why did you go?

American   Well, we lost family.

Alice   . . . Sorry, I'm so sorry, that was so insensitive of me . . .

American   No, no. That's what I was trying to explain earlier. For us this journey is a pilgrimage. Next we're going on to Treblinka . . .

Polish man   Treblinka.

American   . . . Yes to Treblinka, Auschwitz and so on. You know, we felt we had to see . . .

Scene Twenty-seven

Alice *pulls out a spoon. She looks at it. A fast cut to the sitting room of a Polish flat in Warsaw. She is given a bowl of soup. In the same room four* **Students** *watch a game of football. An international match.*

Sister-in-law   Alicia.

Alice Alice.

Alice *(VO)* Arrive in Warsaw.

Sister-in-law Alicia.

Alice Alice.

The **Sister-in-law** *talks to the* **students** *about the game and then addresses* **Alice** *in Polish, asking about herself.*

Sister-in-law Co si stalo?

Student Nie bylo gola.

Sister-in-law Nie bylo gola, o, niech to slag!

Alice Dobre . . . dobre Zupa.

Sister-in-law Typowa Polska zupa. Smakowalo? Tak, bardzo smaczna. Skad jestes, dziecko? Skad. Jestes. Dziecko?

Alice *(VO)* Sister-in-law says . . . .

Sister-in-law Where are you come from?

Alice Always the same question.

Alice *looks out, thinking about the question. Two other memories crowd in. The cab driver (***Simonides***) and another character (the* **Doctor***) we have not yet met. These scenes take place either side of her.*

Simonides Greece.

Doctor Switzerland.

In the taxi.

Simonides Greece, Greece, Hellas, fuck it. I don't miss it. Once I said goodbye to my father's grave it was finished. I sold the house and left. And first I went to Germany. Working in a fucking watch factory.

Doctor *(starts speaking in Swiss)* Sorry, I slipped into my own language. Schwizerdeütsch. Swiss German.

Simonides   After this I came here in London. As you see I work as a minicab driver.

Doctor   You know, I used to look after sheep in the Alps. Now I work for the International Red Cross, that's life for you. I don't think I can help with your father, I've only been here for three weeks.

Simonides   So now I'm British, not Greek, but I don't mind, I don't look back. You know this is the first rule for a taxi driver, don't look back, you will have a crash. No, I am interested in what is in front of me. I believe in the future.

The **Students** *cheer. A goal is almost scored. Cross-fade to the flat. The Polish woman (***Sister-in-law***) mysteriously hands* **Alice** *a box, indicating that it is hers. The woman takes her by the hand and leads her to another room in the flat.* **Virgil** *crosses DSR to television.*

Alice (*VO*)   She gives me a box of his things. A scarf. A lighter. A pair of old shoes. He had small feet. She shows me a bedroom in her flat where he used to lodge when he was a student.

Alice *enters the bleak bedroom.*

She hasn't heard from him for twenty years but she gives me the name of a friend in Riga. How long did he spend in Warsaw? Was he ever on the Baltic coast?

She opens the box.

Scene Twenty-eight

SFX: train cuts the scene. Alice sits with a man, **Daniel***, a BBC foreign correspondent.*

Alice   Well, she wrote down the name of the friend. It's Andrei . . . er . . . Preznez . . . (*Gives up and refers to a piece of paper in the box.*) Andrei Preznezknek.

Daniel (*takes paper*)   Preznezkniac. Preznezkniac. I think you'll find the middle k is silent.

Alice (*taking things out of the box given to her by the* **Sister-in-law**)   Thank you. Shoes.

Daniel   He's a motor cyclist. Well, look at the way the right shoe is worn more than the left. Here and here.

Alice   A lighter.

Daniel   He's a smoker.

Alice   You are brilliant.

Daniel   Thank you.

Alice   And a rather beautiful scarf. That's it.

Daniel   That shouldn't be in there with a pair of shoes and a lighter, it's disrespectful.

Alice   What?

Daniel   It's a tallith.

Alice   No, no it's his scarf.

Daniel   No, it's a tallith. A tallith. A prayer shawl. Do you mind?

He shows her the four corners of the shawl.

These represent the four corners of the world . . . and the knots are the Ten Commandments . . . I think . . . Well that's what I was told. I haven't been to a synagogue since I was a child. Your father is a Jew.

They change seats, holding the scarf between them. As they cross, the **Scientists** *hold out the fragments of wood in the shape of the bow.*

Spindler   His bow had never been used. Not because it was broken, but because it was unfinished. So why did he not complete his bow before he climbed the mountain? His labours must have been disturbed.

Back in the train. When seated **Daniel** *takes the scarf and carefully folds it.* **Alice** *offers him some paper. He gently kisses the scarf. He wraps the scarf in the paper and places it in her bag.*

Alice   I just feel that if I can't trace my past, then I can't relate to people now. As you . . .

Daniel   We are all engaged in the struggle of memory over oblivion. (*Referring to the stone around her neck.*) What is that?

Alice   What? Oh, it's just a rock.

Daniel   Sorry, you were saying. Something about living in the past.

Alice   Yes, if I can't relate to people in the present, I certainly can't fucking imagine a future.

Daniel   Yeah, but you're carrying five thousand years of history, struggle, migration and stories.

Alice   I'm sorry?

Daniel   It's a part of you. You carry it around with you, wherever you are in the world, it's a part of you . . . as a Jew.

Alice   No, no, you've completely misunderstood me.

They change seats, looking at each other as they change. The **Scientists** *change US. They form the shape of the box around* **Virgil***'s cigarette.*

Spindler   The birch bark container, with the comfort from its glowing embers, was the last object that slipped from his fingers. Cold and exhausted. He had been travelling fast.

Back in the train.

Alice   So, you're saying, as a Jew, you hate all Jews.

Daniel   No, it's not as simple as that. I'm saying that, as a Jew, I find Jewish people increasingly impossible to live with.

Alice   That's not what you were saying five minutes ago.

Daniel   That is exactly what I said five minutes ago, if you were listening.

Alice   I was listening. What you're really saying is that you can't live with yourself.

Daniel   He plays the piano.

Alice   What?

Daniel   Your father, he plays the piano. The way the right shoe is worn . . . maybe your father is a pianist.

They change seats, looking more closely at each other as they change. The fragments of wood close in on them from all angles.

Spindler   His quiver was broken and he was carrying the broken pieces as though he had snatched them up in a hurry. All of this tells us that he must have been running . . .

Daniel   Running . . .

Spindler   . . . but what was he running from?

Daniel (*looking out of the window*)   . . . across the whole of Europe, thousands of people running for their lives . . .

Alice   . . . a mass migration . . .

Daniel   Yes, before the Holocaust, before Hitler's Germany, before the twentieth century has even begun. I always think about it every time I travel on this line. They crossed these fields, passed through these villages. It's a great story if you think about it. My four grandparents, all born in different countries. England, Russia, Poland and the Ukraine. As children, in the middle of the night, stuffing a dozen things in a duffel bag and fleeing for their lives. And in a new country finding love, hope and security. It's a beautiful story, an epic story. I just don't know the details. You know, I never bothered to ask. (*Pause.*) It's too late now of course. They're all dead.

Disturbed at his own words he looks at his reflection in the train window. **Alice** *leans forward and attempts to touch him. He senses and turns, laughing.*

Daniel   Er . . . Actually there is something I do know. An old Yiddish drinking song that my grandfather taught me. It's the only cultural baggage I've got. Well, that and the guilt. It's a long journey, and we've got nothing better to do, I'll teach it to you.

Alice   No way.

Daniel   Go on, there's no one on the train.

Alice   No, I can't sing.

Daniel   Well, who can?

Alice   Ella Fitzgerald?

Daniel   No. Ordinary people.

Alice   Lots of people.

Daniel   Go on, no one will hear.

Alice   No.

Daniel   Go on.

Alice   Go on, then.

Daniel   Really? You'll sing with me on a train? Well believe it or not it begins with oy.

Alice   Oy.

Daniel   Yes, oy.

Alice   Oy!

Daniel   No, don't send it up.

He teaches her the song.

Daniel   So the first line is, 'Oy he a vel a volim.' That's woe of woes, a cheery number.

Alice   'Oy he a vel a volim.'

Daniel   'Und die veldt is a cholem.' You need lots of phlegm for that one. Really spit it out.

Alice   'Und die veldt is a cholem.'

Daniel   'Und a xolem is die veldt.' You know, peasants, shtettle, drinking.

Alice   OK. Really drunk. 'Und a xolem is die veldt.'

Daniel   'Und die veldt shtate af geldt.'

Alice   'Und die veldt shtate af geldt.'

Alice *repeats it after him line by line. She sings the last line well.*

Danel   See, you've got a great voice.

Alice   Oh, fuck off.

Daniel   OK. Now we'll sing it together.

*Just as they are about to sing ,***Virgil** *and* **Alice** *are on the phone.*

Virgil   So what happened next?

Alice   We just sang a song.

Virgil   But, Alice, you hate singing.

Back in the train. They both sing. The company join in. As they sing, everyone begins to cross the stage from SR to SL. As they do so, we should be reminded of refugees carrying bags, blankets, chairs.
Simonides *steps behind them, he is in his taxi. The singing continues.*

Simonides   Always moving from east to west. Always running from other fucking people. My grandparents were Greek refugees from Turkey. In 1922 they were expelled, they had to flee. Thousands of people were in the ports, running from the Turkish soldiers, waiting for the boats. My grandmother was on the gangplank. She was carrying her baby in one arm and a watermelon in the other, the only thing she saved. Everybody was pushing and shouting. She was so confused. And this soldier was shouting at her face, 'One item only, you are allowed one object only. Throw this watermelon away.' So she threw it away. She got on the boat and she realised that instead of throwing the watermelon she threw the baby in the sea. But you know, this is the past, my friend, this is the past. I'm going left here, I think it's better. Less traffic on the left. I'm going to emigrate again. Next year I'm going to Melbourne, Australia. The capital of Greece. No, I'm joking. But, you know, Melbourne is the second biggest Greek city in the world. And when I retire I will go to California to get my body frozen so I will wake up stark naked in a better life.

His words echo. **Alice** *is in bed with* **Daniel**. **Virgil** *lies next to* **Alice** *for a moment and then goes to the table and lies on it in despair.*

Alice   What does nakedness remind us of? Dear God, what does nakedness remind us of?

Scene Twenty-nine

Spindler   The Iceman was not naked when he died. He wore grass-filled shoes, leggings, a loin cloth, a shirt, a fur cap and a cloak made from very long grasses. For a man who spent prolonged periods in the wilderness, the construction is marvellous. Easily put on. Easily taken off. Warm, waterproof. For a hunter, moreover, it would provide excellent camouflage. Such a cloak is the mark of an experienced mountaineer. That's what he was, he was an experienced mountaineer.

As **Spindler** *speaks,* **Virgil** *gets off the table, goes to the bed where the lovers are.* **Daniel** *stands up. As* **Virgil** *moves away from the bed, the image of* **Daniel** *and* **Alice** *in bed is repeated.* **Virgil** *stands in his room lost for a moment and then lies on the stone. These movements are repeated like pictures that replay themselves in the sleepless mind, over and over at 4.00 in the morning. Again* **Virgil** *moves from the table, repeating the pattern of movement which continues*

*throughout the following speech. The bed . . . the room . . . falling on
the stone . . . the death. He becomes progressively closer to the stone.*

X-rays of the body reveal to us the violence of his life.
Microanalysis of his right hand reveals injuries sustained
within his last hours. The wounds are defensive wounds
sustained within the last hours of his life, consistent with
close-quarter violent conflict. In that hand he was holding a
knife. So what, or who, was he defending himself against?
Who was he defending himself against?

Again the same movements return.

The X-rays also show a small diamond-shaped shadow deep
in his left shoulder beneath his clavicle. It is a flint
arrowhead. On the back of his shoulder is a fresh entry
wound. The shaft of the arrow had been withdrawn, leaving
the barbed arrowhead deep inside. He was bleeding to
death. He was bleeding to death.

At the end of this final repetition **Virgil**'s *body rests and should
fleetingly remind us of the Iceman's final moments.*

Taken all together, this suggests that the Iceman suffered a
disaster. A fight with hostile humans or with wild animals.
What seems very odd, however, is that he took with him
only some of his equipment. This would suggest that his
presumed adversary did not force him into headlong flight
but, nevertheless, he had to leave the scene in something of
a hurry. This narrows down his opponents to human beings.
Cold, in pain, hungry, pursued. He was fleeing from a
danger, a disaster which provoked him to risk his life.

Virgil *(VO)*   How many children did he have? What word
did he use to signify summer or this place? How many songs
did he know? Had he yet heard the story of the flood?

Virgil *rises from the stone and slowly picks up his phone.*

So who was he, this guy?

Alice   What?

Virgil   What colour was his hair? How long was it?

Alice   I don't know. Brown, nine centimetres long, why do you want to know? . . . Look, for God's sake, it doesn't matter.

Virgil   I just want to know who was he?

Alice   Oh, just some guy I met on the train. He works for the BBC, he's an Eastern Europe correspondent or something. I don't know.

Virgil   BBC Eastern European correspondent. God, Alice, you're so naive. Did you . . . ?

Alice   . . . No. We didn't.

Virgil   No, I mean, didn't you think he might be having you on?

Alice   What?

Virgil   Your father. Maybe it wasn't his.

Alice   What?

Virgil   The tallith. Maybe it wasn't his, maybe someone gave it to him.

Back in the hotel room.

Daniel   I know. It's palaganite. That stone around your neck. It's palaganite. Do you know it's 400 million years old? Give or take the odd fifty million years or so. Mind you, Newtonian time is totally irrelevant. Twenty-four hours is just a human construct which . . .

Alice   Would you like it?

Daniel   What?

Alice   Would you like it?

Daniel   Really?

Alice   Yes, it's too heavy for me.

Daniel Thanks. That's really nice. Have you got the time?

Alice No, my watch is broken.

Daniel Well anyway, what is time after all? It's a fascinating subject. I made a programme about it called *Time*. Maybe you saw it?

Alice No. I didn't.

Daniel It won an award.

Alice *has already left the hotel room and is talking to* **Virgil**.

Alice Of course it's his. I'm sure it's his. I can feel it. If you'd seen all the objects in the box.

Virgil He's just some guy on the train. Why did you believe him?

Alice Virge, don't get stuck on this guy.

Virgil I'm not stuck on this guy. What really happened?

Alice Why do you keep using the word 'really'?

Virgil Because I want to know the truth.

Alice You sound as if you don't believe me.

Virgil Of course I believe you. I just want to know the truth.

Alice You're calling me a liar.

Virgil No, no, I just need to go back over and . . .

Alice I need you to listen to this story. It's very important.

Virgil I'm not sure if what you're saying is real or . . .

Alice I'm just trying to tell you what's happened.

Virgil You're just doing what you always do.

Alice Just listen to me.

Virgil Alice.

Alice   You want to know if I fucked him?

The sound of a train. DS plastic curtain is pulled across.

Scene Thirty

Alice *stands behind the plastic and looks out.* **Virgil** *is in front of the plastic in a similar position.*

Alice   Yes.

Virgil   What?

Alice   No. What does it matter? Can I go on now.

Virgil   Yes.

Alice *fades.* **Virgil** *is left alone.*

Alice (*VO*)   When I get to Riga I take work in a bar. Another fucking bar. This time completely illegally. No papers.

Fast cut to a bar in Riga. We see people dancing. **Virgil** *is still DS of the plastic curtain, smoking a cigarette with one hand almost against the plastic curtain. An image of* **Alice** *dancing in a bar is projected on to the plastic. The image freezes.*

But I track down the friend. An old drunk man. Tells me again and again how I look like him. Same hair too, he says, fingering mine. He tells me jokes all the time. When I laugh, he says, I first heard that one from your father. Again and again and again . . . but I learn I have a half-brother in Kiev. Maybe he's in the Ukraine now.

Everyone crosses the stage, the reverse of the refugees.

South to Kiev. 1,300 miles.

The television flickers into life. Bodies move behind the plastic.

News Broadcast   The remains of a Neolithic man thought to be more than 5,000 years old have arrived at a museum in northern Italy after a journey from Austria in a refrigerated truck.

While **Virgil** *listens to the broadcast the bodies behind the plastic lie down on their chairs, their positions at once suggesting the position of the Iceman and dead bodies in a mortuary.*

The body was moved amid tight security following a threat of unspecified terrorist action by an underground Austrian nationalist group. The discovery of the body a few years ago sparked a dispute between Austria and Italy. This is Daniel Rubens, BBC, Bolzano.

We see the bodies that look almost as if they are suspended in space.

Alice (*VO*)   Kiev. Kiev was desperate. Like chasing shadows. My half-brother isn't there but I meet someone who claims to be my cousin. He works in forensic medicine and says things like:

On the TV, DSR, the close-up of a pair of teeth appear.

Cousin (*VO*)   Alice, you'd be surprised, how much teeth can tell you about a life.

The TV image pulls back to reveal the face of **Spindler**.

Spindler   The teeth of the Iceman are ground down through chewing rather in the manner of a modern-day pipe smoker and the degree of abrasion gives us a clue as to his age which we believe to be between thirty-five and . . .

Virgil   He was forty years old when he died.

Spindler   Which, in the Neolithic period, would have made him an old man.

The image cuts out. Spotlight on **Alice**.

Alice (*VO*)   He gives me a cassette, my father playing the piano, five years ago, New Year's Eve.

The bodies sit up for a moment, briefly evoking the position of a piano player.

Where is he now? My cousin doesn't know but he gives me the name of a hospital near Tarnow in Galicia, Poland, Poland, Poland . . .

Virgil *is on the phone.*

Virgil   A hospital in Poland? My God, what was that like?

A **Doctor** *in a white coat sweeps across to reveal a hospital. He stops by a patient.*

Doctor   So they tell me you're from England.

Alice   Yes, London.

She stands up and walks into the hospital.

Doctor   I am from Switzerland. I used to look after sheep in the Alps, but now I work for the International Red Cross. That's life for you.

Alice   I am looking for my father, I was told you may . . .

The noise obliterates **Alice**'*s words.*

Scene Thirty-one

Doctor (*he speaks Swiss German*)   It's complete chaos here. We have people from everywhere.

Alice   I can't understand you.

Doctor   Sorry, I slipped into my own language. Schwizerdeütsch. Swiss German. I don't know if I can help you. I've only been here for three weeks. It's complete chaos and I'm the only doctor on this ward.

Alice   What the fuck am I supposed to do?

Doctor   Are you OK?

Alice   Please try and help me.

Doctor   Well, there is a woman who has been here for more than a year, maybe she knows something. What was your father's name again?

The noise level obliterates **Alice**'s *reply. A patient clears the plastic and we are in the hospital. A bed rushes into position revealing an old woman propped up on the pillows. The* **Doctor** *speaks to her in German, asking questions. Throughout the following text, she whispers her replies.*

Doctor   She doesn't know the name.

Alice   Shit.

Doctor   Can you tell her anything else about him?

Alice   Well apparently he looked a bit like me. Same hair. Well, it would be grey. He smoked. He played the piano, a jazz pianist. Apparently he was a funny man. Maybe she'd remember that.

The **Doctor** *talks to the woman.*

Alice   What did she say?

Doctor   Apparently there was a man who fits your father's description.

A man comes in and takes away her father's shoe.

Alice   When did he leave? Does she know when he left?

Doctor   Five or six months ago. She's not sure.

Orderly   Doctor. Scand ona yiest? (Where's she from?)

Doctor   London.

Orderly   London. Buckingham Palace. Big Ben.

Doctor   Apparently he had a bad accident.

Alice   An accident?

Doctor   Yes, he broke a few ribs.

A man comes in and takes away her father's lighter. The situation is getting out of control.

Alice   Well, is he alive? Is my father alive? Does she know?

Doctor   One morning he just got up and left. He must have discharged himself.

Orderly   London. Fish and chips.

Alice   Good. Yes. Where is he now? Does she know where he is now?

Doctor   Yes. She does.

A man comes in and takes away her father's tallith.

Doctor   She knows the name of a place called Moklavic.

Alice   Moklavic?

Orderly   Moklavic.

Doctor   It's a village about two or three hours away from here.

Alice   A village?

Orderly   Village people.

Alice   Well how do I get there?

Doctor   You need a car.

Alice   I don't have a car.

Doctor   There's no train going there. You'll need a car. Vitek can take you now, if you really want to go. He's got the time, he's a good driver. You just have to say. Do you want to go? You have to decide now. Do you want to go?

Silence. **Alice** *can't think. She sits on the bed. The noise rises again.* **Virgil** *is on the phone.*

Virgil   Alice? I can hardly hear what you're saying.

Doctor   Please make up your mind. Now.

Alice *tries to get her belongings back. The bed slides sideways as* **Virgil** *moves CS. The break-up of the scene mirrors the voice breaking up over the mobile.*

Virgil   Alice. Alice. You're breaking up. I can only hear one word in three. I can hardly hear what you're saying. Move somewhere else in the room.

Scene Thirty-two

Noise cuts. The scene freezes.

Virgil *(VO)*   Alice? Alice? Shit you've gone completely now. You've fallen off the end of the world. Hello, hello. Alice, I can't hear you any more. Maybe you can hear me. Still can't hear you, still can't hear you. I'll keep talking just in case you can hear me, feel like an idiot. Still here. Got nothing. Got nothing. Alice, oh fuck, if you can hear me, forget everything I've said, I really want you to call me back . . . please.

He looks at the phone. Waits. He switches on the TV and puts the phone on top of it. He goes to the sink, plunges his head in water.

Television *(VO)*   If we look at a map of the weather system, we see air pressures, isobars and winds. These maps look pretty but they're abstract. The normal state of the atmosphere is turbulence and the same is true of the settlement of the earth by human beings. Who can say what caused the Ethiopian drought, hurricane Tracey or the mass migrations which have peopled the earth . . .

Virgil *goes back to the stone and starts to dream.*

Montage *(VO)*   A fairly substantial sample of human hair was recovered from the upper edge of the grass cloak; dark brown, black, curly about nine centimetres long. And in view of his age we may assume that he was balding.

He was balding.

It is highly likely he had a beard.

He had a beard.

And the individual strands of hair point to the fact that he wore his hair loose, not plaited into pigtails or a knot.

He wore his hair loose.

Same hair too, he says, fingering mine.

The dead man's skin is now leathery and tough.

Where is he now?

He lay on his left.

She shows me a room in her flat where he used to lodge as a student.

His head was resting on a boulder. A boulder. He lay down on his left side. He lay on his left.

He had small feet.

For 5,000 years his feet were lying one on top of the other. He lay in a gully to the side of the glacier, so that in 5,000 years the forces in the ice turned him only through ninety degrees.

The four corners of the earth. The ice around him preserved his final gestures. A piano player.

A cloak made from twisted grasses. A lighter. A scarf.

He lay on the rocky ground, fully clothed.

Virgil *looks at the stone. He lifts it, the company fall to the floor. As he moves the stone, the company move as if in the ice. He replaces the stone and the company stand up and continue their journey across the space.*

His objects remained where he placed them . . .

A wind-up watch, Russian-made.

. . . or where they fell from his hands. Broken. Broken. Broken.

Virgil *picks up the chair. It begins to fall apart. He tries to reassemble it.*

It is quite possible for two metres of snow to fall in a single night and snow takes ten or twenty years to turn into ice.

Virgil *(VO)*   And so we can attempt a reconstruction . . .

Alice *(VO)*   Started looking at men over sixty in a different way.

Virgil *begins to move the chair. It suggests an arm, a leg, gestures. He gives up and again it lies flat on the table.*

Montage   What was an old man . . . ?

What was an old man, with arthritic pain . . . ?

What was an old man, with arthritic pain and broken ribs doing . . . ?

What was an old man, with arthritic pain, who had been badly wounded, doing up at 3,000 metres . . . ?

Where are you going?

Was he ever on the Baltic coast? Are you alone?

Where is he now? Where are you now?

What was an old man, with arthritic pain and broken ribs, doing up at 3000 metres with no food at the end of winter?

What are you running from? Where is he now?

Scene Thirty-three

The phone rings.

Virgil   Alice . . . Alice is that you?

*Pause. The sound of **Alice** crying.*

Virgil   Alice, talk to me.

Alice   I need your help.

Virgil   Well, tell me what's happened, what happened after the hospital?

Alice   I can't remember.

Virgil   What?

Alice   I don't remember.

Virgil   What do you mean?

Alice   I just know that there was a car journey. It was cold. There were trees. And then I was on a train here.

Virgil   A train? Where?

Alice   I just had to get out of there. Everywhere I'd been was so flat I needed to get to the mountains.

Virgil   The mountains? What the hell are you talking about?

Alice   I'm in northern Italy.

Virgil   Jesus. Northern Italy? What the fuck are you doing there?

Alice   I'm in some shit hotel.

Virgil   Tell me where you're calling from.

Alice   It's just a small town. Bolzano.

Virgil   Bolzano. I don't believe it. I know it.

Alice   You do?

Virgil   Yes. I've always wanted to go there.

Alice   Why?

Virgil   It's where the Iceman is . . .

Alice   Who?

Virgil   The Iceman, in a museum, in his refrigeration unit. Listen. Sorry. That doesn't matter.

Alice   No, just keep talking, tell me about him. I need to hear your voice.

Virgil   OK. I'll keep talking about the Iceman. Well, do you remember him?

Alice   No.

Virgil   Well, he's the guy they found in 1991 up on the Austrian-Italian border and he was supposed to be five and half a thousand years old? It was in all the papers. There were loads of documentaries about him. Do you remember?

Alice   Vaguely.

Virgil   Well, I got a bit obsessed with him. They found these amazing things about him. They found all these objects and pieced together his life and they discovered that he was an old man and they even found an arrowhead in his shoulder.

Alice   What happened to him?

Virgil   What happened to him? God, there are so many theories . . .

Alice   Well, tell me them.

Scene Thirty-four

Applause. The company enter, quickly, and take their seats in front of the plastic curtain. They are delegates for a conference. They mime ear plugs that give them a simultaneous translation. **Spindler** *is the chairman, he welcomes the audience to the Bolzano conference. We recognise the situation from the first time we saw* **Spindler**.

Spindler   Thank you. Thank you very much. I've been talking for about an hour and a half, so before we close things at the end of this third international conference on

the Iceman in Bolzano I want us to indulge in a little
speculation after all the rigorous scientific debate, and I
want to ask the question, which is always asked of us
involved in the investigation, who was he and what do we
think he was doing up the mountain? So without further ado
let me re-introduce Professor Fitz from Zurich.

Fitz   Ja, danke, darf ich kurz ausholen. Wir haben in
Zürich den Dickdarm des Eismannes untersucht und haben
dabei einen ganz erstaunlichen Fund gemacht, und zwar
haben wir im Stuhlgang Eier des Peitschenwurmes
gefunden. Der Peitschenwurm ist ein Parasit, der den
Menschen vom Schwein her befällt. Somit muss es zur Zeit
des Eismannes schon Hausschweine gegeben haben. Die
hohe Zahl der Eier lässt darauf schliessen, dass der Eismann
an Bauchschmerzen, ja sogar Durchfall gelitten haben muss.
Es ist ja zu komisch, dass gerade wir in der Schweiz uns so
häufig mit Parasiten beschäftigen . . . (*He laughs at his own
joke.*) Wir haben heute in den Tropen etwa acht Millionen
Menschen, die am Peitschenwurm erkrankt sind und
Medikamente gibt es erst seit 1963.

Spindler (*over* **Professor Fitz**)   What he is saying is that
the Iceman had, in his stomach, a worm . . . and that it was
giving him some discomfort . . . and he's just made a joke
about it, it's a bit difficult to translate, it's a Swiss joke.

He hands the microphone to the **Greek Delegate**.

Greek Delegate   Efharisto poli. Ego tha ithela na miliso
gia to halkino tsekouri pou vrethike dipla ston Iceman . . .

The other **Delegates** *indicate that the translation machine no longer
works.*

Greek Delegate   Oh, I'm afraid the translator has
broken. Well, I'll try in English. The Iceman had with him
an axe made from local copper, Alpine copper. This
element is very important. And we found, I mean we the
Greek group, we found in the trichoanalysis, professor, how
do you say trichoanalysis?

Spindler   Analysis of the hair.

Greek Delegate   I love this language, so simple. We found in this trichoanalysis, a high level of copper, and it was local Alpine copper, and we also found that he had black lungs. Why were they black? Because he was smoking a lot of smoke. He was smoking a lot of smoke during the smelting of the copper, so he could be said to be a collector, a smelter and a seller of copper. As a conclusion I would like to say that this man was up there at the top of a mountain because he was a businessman.

English Delegate   A trader.

Greek Delegate   I mean a Neolithic businessman.

English Delegate   A trader.

Greek Delegate   Thank you, Alan.

English Delegate   Thank you. Alan Sheffield, pollen analysis. The pollen on the Iceman reveals traces of summer Alpine flowers from the high regions but also grains which clearly come from the valley in the autumn. So what first comes to mind is transhumance, the seasonal movement of the flock from the mountains in the summer down to the valley in the winter. We can tell from the pollen analysis that he regularly travelled between these altitudes. The area is famous for transhumance of sheep and has been so for at least five thousand years. Now I'm not saying for certain that they are sheep. They could be sheep, they could also be goats, sheep or goats, sheep and goats because sheep and goats get on together very well as a species. They are remarkably loving creatures which brings me to my point, basically, I'm saying that, whatever else he may have been, he was also a shepherd. Thank you.

French Delegate   Merci. Alors, l'homme gelé possédait sur lui un antibiotique naturel, le piptoporus betulinus, ce qui est un fait extraordinaire, c'est un champignon . . .

US Delegate   We can't understand you, I'm afraid.

French Delegate   Oh, sorry. I say that in English. (*Pause.*) So, maybe he was a doctor. Thank you.

US Delegate   Tassle. The tassle. This is the only object on or about the Iceman which can be considered ornamental. It's a very beautiful iridescent marble bead. It is 2.4 centimetres in diameter and it has a hole in the middle. Threaded through the hole is a strip of twisted fur which is knotted. What do these knots represent? It's obvious to me that this is a spiritual object and that the Iceman was quite possibly a shaman which was why he was up the mountain. Mountains are traditionally associated with religious activity and there are many examples of spiritual beads: Greek worry beads, rosary beads etc. But it is very hard for us to understand what a shaman is today so to help us contextualise we could even consider him as an early form of psychiatrist.

English Delegate   Oh, please . . .

US Delegate   It's not that ridiculous. I mean, shamans listen to people. But what I'd really like to talk about here today is violence. Yes, I'd like to discuss the violence in this case because if we're speculating about why this man died up at 3000 metres . . .

English Delegate   Three thousand, two hundred and ten.

US Delegate   Thank you, Alan. Then let us begin by looking at kinship ties and conflict arising from them. This is a patriarchal society – I'm sure the women in the audience will identify with that – and this is an old man, ladies and gentlemen, who leaves his village at a very inappropriate time with broken ribs and is discovered up at 3000 metres with an arrowhead in his left shoulderblade, and defensive fractures of his right fist. What the hell was going on here? Was there some sort of grudge? Was he being forced out? If so, why? Where was his woman? Quite possibly she was not in his bed. I think this is a classic case of clashing Neolithic male egos.

English Delegate   Oh, please . . . .

US Delegate   And, Alan, you should read my book
Neolithic Women.

She is cut off by the general dissent and the **French Delegate** *who
takes the microphone.*

French Delegate   C'est très intéressant de parler de la
violence, et maintenant nous savons une chose, c'est que
notre homme n'est pas mort de faim comme on pouvait le
prétendre . . .

*The microphone is taken from her and it is again explained that the
translation is not working.*

English Delegate   It's broken.

US Delegate   Don't snatch that thing from her . . . now
this is exactly what I'm talking about, ladies and gentlemen.

French Delegate   I'm sorry for your linguistic handicap.
Well. I've completely forgotten what . . .

US Delegate   Is that all you're going to say?

English Delegate   It is pointless speculating about who
or what killed him. There is so little evidence . . .

The microphone is taken by the **Greek Delegate**.

Greek Delegate   I don't quite agree . . .

The microphone is taken by the **Swiss Delegate**.

Swiss Delegate   It is true that he had an arrow in his
shoulder but he also had a worm.

The microphone is taken by **Spindler**. *The* **Delegates** *continue to
argue amongst themselves. During* **Spindler**'*s speech the*
Delegates *sink to the floor and then move steadily across stage.*

Spindler   It is true that there is little empirical evidence as
to the form that violence took in the later Neolithic period.
We can assume that people fought one another, they always
have. Carbon deposits in Neolithic sites suggest that villages

were burned to the ground. We do not know how or why. If
we are to construct a case then we have to look for a parallel
example and in this case there is one. A shocking example.
In Talheim in southwest Germany, in 1983, are the ruins of
a Neolithic settlement. On the edge of the village was a mass
grave. More than half the bodies were lying on their
stomachs, their arms and legs sticking out at absurd angles
in defiance of anatomy. Each one wedged on top of another.
Everyone had been murdered.

*There is a switch to a recorded voice and the company crouch down
revealing a dual image of* **Virgil** *in his room and the Iceman reaching
his resting place.*

Spindler (*VO*)   Some of the blows had been administered
whilst the bodies were upright. Others while the dying were
lying on the ground. As there are no defensive fractures, one
may assume a regular execution. Afterwards the bodies were
carelessly tossed into a pit. The community of dead
represent the complete population range of a Neolithic
village. Men, old men and women, children too. It is
conceivable that a fate similar to that of Talheim also befell
the Iceman's native village. In a hopeless situation he
succeeded in fleeing from the enemy . . .

Scene Thirty-five

The company exit. Behind the plastic the light comes up on **Virgil**,
now on his bed. His voice merges with **Spindler**'s.

Virgil (*VO*)   In a hopeless situation he succeeded in fleeing
from the enemy. Every effort was made to capture him. If,
as we know from Talheim, even women and children were
massacred, how much more dangerous would a grown
man's escape from the pogrom seem to the victors. His only
advantage was his superior local knowledge. There was no
hope of return at whatever time and for whatever purpose.
So the man set out in the direction of Hauslabjoch hoping

that beyond the main ridge of the Alps he might escape his pursuers.

The company enter. Over the following text, the chair slowly becomes the puppet of the Iceman. The company manipulate him. He has a stick and his face is suggested by a towel. The puppet of the Iceman follows the final moments of the Iceman in his gully, five thousand years ago. First he gets off the table.

Overtaken by a blizzard or sudden fog, the Iceman was in a state of total exhaustion. (*He bends and goes on.*) In the gully in the rock, perhaps familiar to him from previous crossings of the pass, he sought what shelter he could from the bad weather. With his failing strength he settled down for the night. (*He rests on* **Virgil***'s TV and takes the stick in his other hand.*) He deposited his axe on the ledge of a rock. (*He moves towards the bed.*)

Meanwhile it had grown dark. It was snowing ceaselessly and an icy cold penetrated his clothes. A terrible fatigue engulfed his limbs. He knew that to fall asleep meant death.

(*His hat flies off.*) He staggered forward a few more steps. He slipped and fell against a rock. (*He falls.*) The birch bark container fell from his hand; his cap fell off.

(*He falls to his knees, his head falls against the stone.*) He only wanted a short rest but his need for sleep was stronger than his will power. He laid his head on the rock. Soon his clothes froze to the rough ground. He was no longer aware that he was freezing to death.

The puppet by now is lying on the stone. The only movements are its final breaths. The company slowly retreat from the body. **Virgil***'s voice comes off VO and the audience are aware that he is now speaking on the mobile phone to* **Alice***. Her face can be seen in the two-way mirror.*

Alice   So is that what happened?

Virgil   How can we know? Who can say? It's just one theory. A way of getting closer. A story. We need stories.

Alice I need my story.

Virgil Alice, tell me what happened.

Alice I can't.

Virgil Why?

Alice Because I didn't go.

Virgil Go where?

Alice My father's village. I couldn't go. And now I'll never know.

Virgil Why do you need to know?

Alice Because if I don't know, I feel I can't come home.

Virgil Then imagine.

Alice What?

Virgil Imagine.

Pause.

Alice In the village there is an apple orchard. It's a sunny afternoon. And I find him asleep between the trees. One hand open on the grass, palm upwards, the other under his back. I can tell you everything about his face. I don't wake him up. Virge. Are you still there?

Virgil Yes I'm here. I've been here for nine months.

Alice What are you wearing?

Virgil What kind of question is that?

Alice I just want to know.

Virgil A T-shirt and trousers.

Alice Do I know them?

Virgil No . . .

Alice Well, take them off.

Virgil   What?

Alice   Take them off.

Virgil   Why?

Alice   Because it reminds me.

Virgil   All right. I'll do it. Wait there. Don't go anywhere. Crazy woman.

He takes off his clothes and gets on to the bed.

Alice   That way I can see you.

Virgil   OK. I've got them off, what do you want me to do now?

Alice   I just want you to talk to me. Tell me what you're doing.

Virgil   Well that's easy enough because I'm just sitting on my bed . . .

The call starts to break up and we can no longer hear him.

Alice   You're beginning to break up . . .

Virgil   . . . and in a few minutes I'm going to make myself a . . .

Alice   Hello, hello . . . ? Virge, can you hear me? I don't know if you can hear me. If you can hear me, I'll go and see the Iceman tomorrow and tell you what he's like. And please ring me back. (*Pause.*) I'd like that.

Scene Thirty-six

Virgil *also realises that they have been cut off. He tries to call her back. Fails. He gets up and looks in the mirror.* **Alice** *can still be seen behind it. She fades slowly as he looks at her. When* **Alice**'s *voice begins we should be uncertain for a moment whether it is in her mind or* **Virgil**'s.

Alice *(VO)*   What does nakedness remind us of? Dear God, what does nakedness remind us of? Naked, our needs are so clear, our fears so natural.

Virgil *stands alone in front of the table in his room.*

Alice *(VO)*   There is nothing innocent about the naked. Only the newborn are innocent. Seeing a naked body of any age we remember our own, putting ourselves in someone else's place, in the gully, for example, five thousand years ago.

He lies on the table evoking the dual image we have seen throughout the piece. When alone at the beginning, as the Iceman in the forensic lab, as himself imagining **Alice** *with the other man, the BBC correspondent.*

Seeing a naked body of another person we make an inventory of our own.

The other company members appear silently behind the table and hold up the metal frame of the Iceman's refrigeration unit in front of them. They are looking at him in his museum in Bolzano. **Alice** *joins them. Through her VO we begin to understand they are looking at him not with mere ghoulish curiosity, not in horror, but with empathy.*

Shoulderblade, ribs, clavicle. We list the sensations we feel in each part, one by one, all of them indescribable, all of them familiar, all of them constituting a home.

Suddenly, strangely, one of the people behind the frame slips under it and continues towards the Iceman as if drawn into his presence. In one moment they have changed places. The man watching is on the table. He has put himself in the Iceman's place, and the Iceman has become **Virgil** *again.*

Then one by one the members of the company follow each other in lying in the place of the Iceman. They lay themselves down and roll off again just as generation succeeds generation in a never-ending cycle.

Alice *(VO)*   All of them indescribable.

Virgil *(VO)*   All of them indescribable.

Alice (*VO*)   All of them familiar.

Virgil (*VO*)   All of them familiar.

Alice (*VO*)   All of them constituting a home.

Virgil (*VO*)   All of them constituting a home.

Alice (*VO*)   Constituting a home.

Virgil (*VO*)   Constituting a home.

Alice (*VO*)   A home.

Virgil (*VO*)   A home.

The words echo. The rolling becomes quicker and quicker. The bed and the sink slide offstage as the image becomes concentrated on these continuously rolling, tumbling bodies. They are back-lit now by neons, the entire width of the stage, and you can only see them in silhouette. Underneath there are the repeating mantra-like voices of all the company . . .

Montage (*VO*)   A broken stick. Splinters of wood. Scraps of leather. Fur. Tufts of twisted grass. Strips of hide. Fragments of birch bark. A broken stick. Two round objects on a piece of twine.

Finally the last company member rolls over the table. The table itself hurtles offstage. The neons rise and clear. The company form a line DS. They lean forward as if about to take a step. Their silhouettes briefly evoke the photographs of Muybridge. From standing they lean back as if assessing the size of a mountain in front of them. Suddenly their heads snap sideways. What have they seen? The gully? A parent? The future? The audience now becomes aware of a huge projection of the Iceman, emerging on to the back plastic. The company turn towards it. They walk upstage towards the body of the Iceman. Before they get there . . .

Fade to black.